EXCAVATIONS AND SURVEYS
IN SOUTHERN RHODES:
THE MYCENAEAN PERIOD

PUBLICATIONS OF THE NATIONAL MUSEUM

Archaeological Historical Series Vol. XXII: I

RESULTS OF THE CARLSBERG FOUNDATION EXCAVATIONS
IN RHODES 1902–1914

LINDOS IV, 1

EXCAVATIONS AND SURVEYS IN SOUTHERN RHODES: THE MYCENAEAN PERIOD

by

SØREN DIETZ

THE NATIONAL MUSEUM OF DENMARK

1984

Printed in Denmark by
AiO Print Ltd., Odense
Copyright © 1984 Nationalmuseet
ISBN 87-480-0487-1

Contents

Frontispiece 1. Jug 4,2 (1st. inv. no. 4248) from Passia grave 4. Watercolour by Helvig Kinch. 1 : 2

Frontispiece 2. Jar 4,5 (1st. inv. no. 4243) from Passia grave 4. Watercolour by Helvig Kinch. 1 : 2.

Preface

The Danish excavations on southern Rhodes, sponsored by the Carlsberg Foundation, concentrated mainly on the Lindos Acropolis and surrounding town. However, quite extensive field work was simultaneously carried out by K. F. Kinch in other places in the southern part of the island. The co-director, Chr. Blinkenberg, only spent shorter periods in Rhodes during the work at Lindos itself, and he never returned to the island after 1905.

The most important of the investigations outside Lindos was the excavation in 1907 of the commercial port of Vroulia at the southernmost tip of the island, which was published by K. F. Kinch in 1914[1]. A considerable Geometric cemetery at Exochi, excavated in 1914, was later published by K. Friis Johansen[2]. The antiquities found by the Danish expedition were shared between the museum in Istanbul and that in Copenhagen, where the diaries, field notes and plans are now kept[3].

The final publication of the results of the excavations appeared to be E. Dyggve's (and V. Poulsen's) large volume on the architecture (and sculpture) of Lindos, 1960[4]. However, a renewed study of the archives by my colleague Mr. S. Trolle in 1971 disclosed that Chr. Blinkenberg had planned to include quite an amount of material and information in a final volume, but this never materialised before his death.

The present volume, which should thus be considered the final in the series, is divided into two sections. The first and present one deals with the Mycenaean material excavated and collected by Kinch, supplemented with survey material brought to light during the summer of 1975. The text is based on a preliminary manuscript by Kinch, but not finished before his death in 1921, as well as on information from his diaries. The majority of the pottery excavated by Kinch is now in the Archaeological Museum in Istanbul, while items of metal, stone, glass, etc., are mostly kept in the National Museum, Copenhagen. The second section, to be published by S. Trolle, L. Wriedt Sørensen and M.-L. Buhl, will deal with the remaining material from the historical periods. Furthermore it will include the measurements of the Medieval buildings of Lindos prepared for publication by the architect Cathrine Gerner.

The Istanbul pottery was studied in 1974 and surveys were carried out on Rhodos in 1975. We are most grateful to the Carlsberg Foundation for defraying all the expenses connected with these activities and with the preparation of the material. Moreover, the Foundation generously granted funds for publishing both sections of the present volume.

For permission to study and publish the Istanbul material, we are most obliged to the former director of the Archaeological Museum, Dr. N. Dulunay, as also to Dr. N. Firatli and Miss Tulay Ergil, who all helped and facilitated our studies in every possible way. We are likewise very grateful to the successive ephors of Rhodes, Dr. C. Doumas and Dr. Ioannis Papachristodoulou and their staff. Throughout the time we spent on Rhodes, we enjoyed extraordinary kindness and interest in our work. Several other friends and colleagues contributed with help and advice. First and foremost, I should like to thank my colleague Mr. Steffen Trolle for his excellent assistance during the work and Mr. Henrik Frost for taking most of the photographs and preparing them for publication. In Athens in 1978 Dr. C. Mee generously shared his profound knowledge of Mycenaean Rhodes with me and readily, throughout the years, he has put his various publications at my disposal.

If the present work should be stamped by an "Argivocentric" starting-point, this is undoubtedly a result of my earlier activities in the Argolid. I am greatly indebted to "Argive" friends from those years, and in particular to Dr. Lisa French, Dr. Klaus Kilian and Dr. Chr. Podzuweit for their constant interest in my work and much good advice.

The majority of the drawings were partly drawn or redrawn by Cathrine Gerner MAA; furthermore Mr. Johs. Frederiksen and Mr. Finn Beltov MAA provided lay-outs and a few drawings. The manuscript was typed by Mrs. Marianne Willumsgaard and Mrs. Connie Villemoes. The text was revised by Mrs. Jennifer Paris, Wales. To all I am greatly indebted.

National Museum, Copenhagen.
January 1984.

List of Figures

Fig. 103. Stirrup jar 1,13 (Ist. inv.no. 4619) from Granto grave 1. Seen from the side and from above. 1 : 2.

Fig. 104. Stirrup jar no. 1,15 (Ist. inv.no. 4620) from Granto grave 1. Seen from the side and from above. 1 : 2.

Fig. 105. Stirrup jar no. 1,18 (Ist. inv.no. 4621) from Granto grave 1. Seen from the side and from above. 1 : 2.

Fig. 106. Flat cup no. 1,19 (Ist. inv.no. 4623) from Granto grave 1. 1 : 2.

Fig. 107. Ta Tzingani (Kattavia) grave a (from Kinch's sketchbook). N to the right.

Fig. 108. One-edged knife no. 1 from the chamber tomb at Ta Tzingani (Copenhagen inv.no. 7700). Photo and drawing. 1 : 2.

Fig. 109. Fish hook (Copenhagen inv.no. 7701) from Mycenaean grave at Kattavia. 1 : 1.

Fig. 110. Two necklaces from Kattavia (Copenhagen inv.nos. 7702 and 7703). 1 : 2.

Fig. 111. Rim sherd of deep bowl from Rhodes (Copenhagen inv.no. 7566). 1 : 2.

Fig. 112. A carnelian bead from Mallona and two gold rosettes having Rhodes as provenance. (Copenhagen inv.no. 7704 and 7706). 1 : 1.

Fig. 113. Kylix having Rhodes as provenance (Copenhagen inv.no. 12364). 1 : 2.

Fig. 114. Stirrup jar having Rhodes as provenance (Copenhagen inv.no. 12501). Seen from the side and from above. 1 : 2.

Fig. 115. Stirrup jar having provenance "Lindos SW above town, 21/4–14". Yaltos. (Copenhagen inv.no. 12502). 1 : 2.

Fig. 116. Sections of stirrup jars in chronological sequence. 1 : 5.

Fig. 117. Sections of storage jars in chronological sequence. Scales 1 : 5 and 1 : 10 (note that Passia 4,10 should be Passia 1,10).

Fig. 118. Sections of jugs. 1 : 5.

Fig. 119. Sections of kraters. 1 : 5.

Fig. 120. Sections of various open bowls and cups. 1 : 2.

Fig. 121. Sections of kylikes and deep bowls. 1 : 5.

Fig. 122. Stirrup jar purchased in Italy (Copenhagen inv.no. 8696). Seen from the side and from above. 1 : 2.

Bibliography

(For abbreviations I follow the American Journal of Archaeology 82, 1978 with addenda and corrigenda in *AJA* 84, 1980).

Acts of The International Archaeological Symposium "The Mycenaeans in the Eastern Mediterranean", Nicosia 1973.

Acts of The International Archaeological Symposium "The Relations Between Cyprus and Crete, Ca. 2000–500 B.C.", Nicosia 1979.

Anson D., "The Rude Style Late Cypriot IIC-III Pottery : An Analytical Typology", *OpusAth* XIII, 1980, p. 1ff.

Barber R. L. N., "The Late Cycladic Period : a Review", *BSA* 76, 1981, pp. 1–21.

Bass G. F., *Cape Gelidonya : A Bronze Age Shipwreck*. Philadelphia 1967.

Benzi M., "Tombe micenee di Rodi riutilizzate nel TE IIIC", *SMEA* 23, 1982, pp. 323–336.

Biancofiore F., *La Civiltà Micenea nell'Italia Meridionale* I, *La Ceramica*, Roma 1963.

Blegen C. W., *Zygouries. A Prehistoric Settlement in the Valley of Cleonae*, Cambridge, Mass. 1928.

– , *Prosymna : The Helladic Settlement Preceding the Argive Heraeum*, Cambridge, Mass. 1937, vol. I-II.

Blegen C. W., Caskey J. L., Rawson M., *Troy, The Sixth Settlement*, Connecticut 1953, vol. III (1–2).

– , *Troy Settlements VIIa, VIIb and VIII*, Connecticut 1958, vol. IV (1–2).

Blinkenberg Chr. et Friis Johansen K., *CVA* Danemark, Fasc. 1, Copenhague : Musée National, Fasc. 1.

Blinkenberg Chr. et Friis Johansen K., *CVA* Danemark, Fasc. 1, Copenhague : Musée National, Fasc. 2.

Boardman J., *The Cretan Collection in Oxford. The Dictaean Cave and the Iron Age Crete*, Oxford 1961.

Broneer O., "A Mycenaean Fountain on the Athenian Agora", *Hesperia* 8, 1939, pp. 317–433.

Buchholz H.-G., "Kriegswesen, Teil 2", *Archaeologia Homerica* I, E, 2 Göttingen 1980 (mit Beiträgen von Stephan Foltiny und Olaf Höckmann).

Buchholz H.-G., Jöhrens G. und Maull J., "Jagd und Fischfang", *Archaeologia Homerica* I, J. Göttingen 1973.

Cadogan G., "Late Minoan IIIC Pottery from the Kephala Tholos Tomb near Knossos", *BSA* 62, 1962, pp. 257 ff.

Caskey J. L., "Investigations in Keos, Part II : A Conspectus of the Pottery", *Hesperia* 41, 1972, pp. 357–401.

Catling H. W., "Late Minoan Vases and Bronzes in Oxford", *BSA* 63, 1968, p. 89–131.

Catling H. W. (ed), "Archaeology in Greece, 1981–82", *JHS-AR* 28, 1981–82.

Cavanagh W. and Mee C., "The re-use of earlier Tombs in the LHIIIC period", *BSA* 73, 1978, pp. 31–44.

Desborough V. d'A, *The Last Mycenaeans and their Successors. An Archaeological Survey c. 1200-c. 1000 B.C.*, Oxford 1964.

Deshayes J., *Argos, Les Fouilles de la Deiras*, Paris 1966 (Études Péloponnésiennes, IV).

Despini G., "Ἀνασκαφὴ Τήνου", *Praktika* 1979, pp. 228–235.

Dietz S. and Trolle S., *Arkæologens Rhodos*, Kbhvn. 1974.

– , "Rhodos 70 år efter –", *Nationalmuseets Arbejdsmark* 1976, pp. 61–71.

Dietz S., "General Stratigraphical Analysis and Architectural Remains", *Asine* II, 1. Sthlm. 1982.

Dikaios P., *Enkomi, Excavations 1948–1958*, Vol. IIIa, Mainz 1969.

Dyggve E. and Poulsen V., *Lindos, Fouilles de l'Acropole 1902–1914 et 1952*, Berl./Copenh. 1960.

Forsdyke E. J., "Prehistoric Aegean Pottery", *Catalogue of the Greek and Etruscan Vases in the British Museum*, Vol. I, Part I. London 1925.

French E., "Late Helladic IIIA 1 Pottery from Mycenae", *BSA* 59, 1964, p. 241 ff.

– , "Late Helladic IIIA 2 Pottery from Mycenae", *BSA* 60, 1965, p. 159 ff.

– , "A Group of Late Helladic IIIB 1 Pottery from Mycenae", *BSA* 61, 1966, p. 216 ff.

– , "Pottery from Late Helladic IIIB 1 Destruction Contexts at Mycenae", *BSA* 62, 1967, p. 149 ff.

– , "A Group of Late Helladic IIIB 2 Pottery from Mycenae", *BSA* 64, 1969, p. 71 ff.

– , "The first Phase of LH IIIC", *AA* 1969, pp. 133–136.

– , "The Development of Mycenaean Terracotta Figurines", *BSA* 66, 1971, pp. 101–187.

– , "A Reassessment of the Mycenaean Pottery at Tarsus", *AS XXV*, 1975, pp. 53–75.

Friis-Johansen K., "Exochi, ein frührhodisches Gräberfeld", *ActaA* 28, 1958, pp. 1–192.

Frizell B. Santillo, "The Late Mycenaean Periods", *Asine* II, 3 (Forthcoming).

Frödin O. and Persson A. W., *Asine. Results of the Swedish Excavations 1922–1930*, Sthlm. 1938.

Furtwaengler A. and Loeschke G., *Mykenische Vasen, vorhellenische Thongefässe aus dem Gebiet des Mittelmeeres*. Berlin 1886.

Furumark A., *The Mycenaean Pottery, Analysis and Classification*, Sthlm. 1941.

– , *The Chronology of Mycenaean Pottery*, Sthlm. 1941.

– , "The Mycenaean IIIC Pottery and its Relation to Cypriote Fabrics", *OpusArch*. Vol. III, 1944, pp. 194–265.

14

Gjerstad E., "The Initial Date of the Cypriote Iron Age", *OpusArch*. Vol. III, 1944, pp. 73–106.

Hanfmann G. M. A. and Waldbaum J. C., "Two Submycenaean Vases and a Tablet from Stratonikeia in Caria", *AJA* 72, 1968, p. 51 ff.

Hankey V. and Warren P., "The Absolute Chronology of the Aegean Late Bronze Age". *BICS* 21, 1974, pp. 142–152.

Harden D. B., *Catalogue of Greek and Roman Glass in the British Museum*, Vol. I, London 1981.

Hiller S., *Alt-Ägina*, IV, 1, *Mykenische Keramik*, Mainz 1975.

Hood S., *Excavations in Chios 1938–1955, Prehistoric Emporio and Ayio Gala*, Vol. II. Oxford 1982.

Hood S., Huxley G. and Sandars N. K., "A Minoan Cemetery on Upper Gypsades", *BSA* 53–54, 1958–1959, pp. 194–262.

Hope Simpson R. and Lazenby J. F., Notes from the Dodecanese III, *BSA* 68, 1973, pp. 127–179.

Hope Simpson R. and Dickinson O. T. P. K., "A Gazetteer of Aegean Civilisation in the Bronze Age, Vol. I : The Mainland and the Islands", *SIMA* vol. LII, Göteborg 1979.

Hägg I and R., *Excavation in the Barbouna Area at Asine*, Fasc. 2, Uppsala 1978.

Hägg R. and Marinatos N. (eds.), *Sanctuaries and Cults in the Aegean Bronze Age*. Sthlm. 1981. (Skrifter utgivna av Svenska Inst. i Athen 4°, XXVIII).

Höckmann O., "Lanze und Speer im spätminoischen und mykenischen Griechenland", *JRGZM* 27, 1980, pp. 13–158.

Iakovidis S. E., "Περατή, το νεκροταφείον", Ath. 1972.

– , "On the Use of Mycenaean 'Buttons'", *BSA* 72, 1977, pp. 113–119.

Inglieri R. U., *Carta Archeologica dell'Isola di Rodi*, Firenze 1936.

Jacopi G., "Nuovi scavi nella necropoli micenea di Ialisso", *ASAtene* XIII-XIV (1930–31), Bergamo 1933, pp. 253–345.

– , "Sepolcreto micenea di Calavarda" in *ClRh* 6–7, 1932–33, p. 133–150.

– , *CVA* Italia, Fasc X, Rodi-Fasc. II.

Jones R. E. and Mee C., "Spectrographic Analysis of Mycenaean Pottery from Ialysos on Rhodes : Results and Implications", *JFA* vol. 5, no. 4, 1978, pp. 461–470.

Kanta A., *The Late Minoan III Period in Crete. A Survey of Sites, Pottery and their Distribution*. Göteborg 1980 (*SIMA* LVIII).

Karageorghis V., *Nouveaux Documents pour l'Étude du Bronze Récent a Chypre, recueil critique et commenté* (Ecole Française d'Athènes, Études Chypriotes III). Paris 1965.

– , *Excavations at Kition I. The Tombs*. Nicosia 1974.

– , *Alaas, A Protogeometric Necropolis in Cyprus*. Nicosia 1975.

Karageorghis V., *Cyprus from the Stone Age to the Romans*, London 1982.

Kilian K. et al., "Ausgrabungen in Tiryns 1976", *AA* 1978 pp. 449–498.

– , "Ausgrabungen in Tiryns 1977", *AA* 1979, pp. 379–458.

Kilian K., "Zum Ende der mykenischen Epoche in der Argolis", *JRGZM* 27. Jahrg. 1980, pp. 166–195.

– , "Ausgrabungen in Tiryns 1978, 1979", *AA* 1981, pp. 149–256.

– , "Ausgrabungen in Tiryns 1981", *AA* 1983, pp. 277–328.

Kinch K. F., *Fouilles de Vroulia*, Berlin 1914.

Konstantinopoulos Gr., "Νέα ευρήματα εκ Ρόδου και Αστυπαλαίας", *AAA* 6, 1973, pp. 114–120.

Kraiker W. und Kübler K., "Die Nekropolen des 12. bis 10. Jahrhunderts", *Kerameikos. Ergebnisse und Ausgrabungen* I, Berlin 1939.

MacNamara E., "A group of Bronzes from Surbo, Italy : new evidence for Aegean contacts with Apulia during Mycenaean IIIB and C. *ProcPS* 36, 1970, pp. 241–260.

Maiuri A., "Ialisos, scavi della Missione Archeologica Italiana a Rodi", *ASAtene* VI-VII, pp. 83–256. Bergamo 1926.

Marinatos S., "Kleidung – Haar und Barttracht", *Archaeologia Homerica* I, A. Göttingen 1967.

Mee C., *The Dodecanese in the Bronze Age*, (Diss. 1975).

– , "Aegean Trade and Settlement in Anatolia in the Second Mill. B. C.", *AS* XXVIII, 1978, p. 121–156.

– , *Rhodes in the Bronze Age*, Warminster 1982.

Milojčic Vl., "Einige mitteleuropäische Fremdlinge auf Kreta", *JRGZM* 2, 1955, pp. 153–169.

Montelius O., *La Grece Préclassique*, Sthlm. 1924.

Morricone L., "Eleonae e Langada: Sepolcreti della tarda Età del Bronzo a Coo", *ASAtene* NS 27–28, Roma 1967, p. 5 ff.

– , "Coo-Scavi e scoperte nel "Serraglio" e in località minori (1935–43)", *ASAtene* vol. L-LI (NS XXXIV-XXXV (1972–73)). Roma 1975.

Pantelidou M. A., "Αι προιστορικαι Αθηναι", Ath. 1975.

Papadopoulos Th. J., *Mycenaean Achaea*, SIMA LV, 1978/79.

Papadopoulos Th. J. and Jones R. E., "Rhodiaka in Achaea", *OpusAth*. XIII, 1980, p. 225 ff.

Podzuweit Chr., "Spätmykenische Keramik von Kastanas", *JRGZM* 26, 1979, pp. 203–223.

– , "Die mykenische Welt und Troja", *Südosteuropa zwischen 1600 und 1000 v. Chr.* (Prähistorische Archäologie in Südosteuropa), Berlin 1982, pp. 65–88.

– , "Bericht zur spätmykenischen Keramik", *AA* 1983, pp. 359–402.

Popham M., "Some Late Minoan III Pottery from Crete", *BSA* 60, 1965, pp. 316–342.

– , "Late Minoan IIIB Pottery from Knossos", *BSA* 65, 1970, pp. 195–202.

– , "The Destruction of the Palace at Knossos", Göteborg 1970. *SIMA* XII.

Popham M. and Milburn E., "Late Helladic IIIC Pottery of Xeropolis (Lefkandi), A Summary", *BSA* 66, 1971, pp. 333–352.

Rudolf W., "Die Nekropole am Prophitis Elias bei Tiryns", *Tiryns VI*, pp. 23–126 ff. 8–56. Mainz 1973.

Rutter J. B., "Late Helladic IIIC Pottery and Some Historical Implications", *Symposium on the Dark Ages in Greece*, N.Y. 1977, pp. 1–20. (Davis E. J. (ed.)).

– , "The Last Mycenaeans at Corinth", *Hesperia* 48, 1979, p. 348 ff.

Sandars N. K., "The Antiquity of the One-edged Bronze Knife in the Aegean", *ProcPS* 20, 1955, pp. 174–197.

– , "Later Aegean Bronze Swords", *AJA* 67, 1963, pp. 118–153.

– , *The Sea Peoples, Warriors of the Ancient Mediterranean 1250–1150*, London 1978.

Schachermeyr F., *Die Mykenische Zeit und die Gesittung von Thera*, (Die Ägäische Frühzeit II) Wien 1976.

– , *Kreta zur Zeit der Wanderungen vom Ausgang der minoischen Ära bis zur Dorisierung der Insel*, (Die Ägäische Frühzeit III) Wien 1979.

– , *Griechenland im Zeitalter der Wanderungen. Vom Ende der mykenischen Ära bis auf die Dorier*, (Die Ägäische Frühzeit IV) Wien 1980.

Schaeffer C. F. A., *Ugaritica* II, Paris 1949.

– , *Ugaritica* VII, Paris 1978.

Schilardi D., "Ανασκαφὲς στὴν Πάρο", *Praktika* 1977, pp. 363–377.

15

– , "The destruction of the Mycenaean Citadel at Koukounaries on Paros", Davis J. L. and Cherry J. F., (eds.) *Papers in Cycladic Prehistory* 1979, pp. 158–78.

Sherratt E. S., "Regional Variations in the Pottery of the Late Helladic IIIB", *BSA* 75, 1980, p. 175 ff.

Smith A. H., *CVA*, Great Britain, Fasc. 1, British Museum, fasc. 1, London 1925.

Spyropoulos Th. G., "Αωασκαφὴ Μνκηναικῆς Τανάγρας", *Praktika* 1979 (1981), p. 27 ff.

– , "Υστερομυκηναικοί ελλαδικοι θησαυροι" Athens 1972.

Stubbings F. H., *Mycenaean Pottery from the Levant*. Cambridge 1951.

Styrenius C.-G., *Submycenaean Studies*, Lund 1967.

Theocharis D., "Ο τύμβος τον Εξαλόφου και ή εισβολή τω Θεσσαλών" *AAA* 1, 1968, pp. 289–294.

Tzedakis I., "Ανασκαφὴ εις Αρμένους Ρεθύμνης", *Deltion* 26 (1971), 1975, pp. 513–516.

Verdelis N., French E. and D. "Μνκηναικὴ επιχωσις εξωθεν του δντικου τειχους της ακροπόλεως", *Deltion* 20 (1965) A, 1966, p. 137–152.

Vermeule E. and Karageorghis V., *Mycenaean Pictorial Vase Painting*, Cambridge et. al. 1982.

Voigtländer W., "Tiryns, Unterburg-Kampagne 1972", *AAA* VI, 1973, pp. 28–38.

– , "Zur Chronologie der spätmykenischen Burgen bei Tiryns", *Tiryns* VI, Berl. 1973, pp. 241–266.

Wace A. J. B. et. al., "Excavations at Mycenae", *BSA* 25, 1921–22, 1922–23.

Wace A. J. B., *Chamber Tombs at Mycenae, Archaeologia*, Vol. LXXXII, Oxford 1932.

Walters H. B., "Cypriote, Italian and Etruscan Pottery". *Catalogue of the Greek and Etruscan Vases in the British Museum*. Vol. I, Part II, London 1912.

Walters H. B. and Forsdyke E. J., *CVA*, Great Britain, Fasc. 7, British Museum, Fasc. 5, London 1930.

Wardle K. A., "A Group of Late Helladic IIIB 1 Pottery from Mycenae", *BSA* 64, 1969, pp. 261 ff.

– , "A Group of Late Helladic IIIB 2 Pottery from Mycenae", *BSA* 68, 1973, pp. 297–348.

Wells B., "The Protogeometric Period", *Asine* II, 4, 2–3, Sthlm. 1983.

Yalouris N., "An Unreported Use for Some Mycenaean Glass Paste Beads", *JGS* X, 9–16, 1968.

Zervoudaki I., "Αρμενοχώρι", *Deltion* 26, 1971, pp. 550–551, PPs. 558–560.

Åström P., "Cyprus and Troy", *OpusAth*. XVIII:3, 1980, pp. 23–28.

Åström P., Bailey D. N. and Karageorghis V., *Hala Sultan Tekke* I, Göteborg 1976, (*SIMA* XLV:1).

List of Abbreviations

Acts Nicosia 1972, *Acts of the International Archaeological Symposium "The Mycenaeans in the Eastern Mediterranean"*, Nicosia 27th March-2nd April 1972. Nicosia 1973.

Acts Nicosia 1978, *Acts of the International Archaeological Symposium "The Relations Between Cyprus and Crete, ca. 2000–500 B. C."*, Nicosia 16th April-22nd April 1978. Nicosia 1979.

Ägäische Frühzeit II Schachermeyr F., *Die mykenische Zeit und die Gesittung von Thera*, Wien 1976.

Ägäische Frühzeit III Schachermeyr F., *Kreta zur Zeit der Wanderungen vom Ausgang der minoischen Ära bis zur Dorisierung der Insel*, Wien 1979.

Ägäischen Frühzeit IV Schachermeyr F., *Griechenland im Zeitalter der Wanderungen. Vom Ende der mykenischen Ära bis auf die Dorier*, Wien 1980.

Arkæologens Rhodos Dietz S. and Trolle S., *Arkæologens Rhodos*, København 1974.

Asine I Frödin O. and Persson A. W., *Asine. Results of the Swedish Excavations 1922–1930*, Sthlm. 1938.

Asine II For the volumes in this series see : Dietz S., *Asine II, Results of the Excavations East of the Acropolis 1970–1974*. Fasc. 1, "General Stratigraphical Analysis and Architectural Remains", Sthlm. 1982.

Barbouna 2 Hägg I. and R., (eds.), *Excavations in the Barbouna Area at Asine*, Fasc. 2. Uppsala 1978.

BMCat 1,1 Forsdyke E. J., "Prehistoric Aegean Pottery", *Catalogue of the Greek and Etruscan Vases in the British Museum*, Vol. I. Part I., London 1925.

BMCat 1,2 Walters H. B., "Cypriot, Italian and Etruscan Pottery", *Catalogue of the Greek and Etruscan Vases in the British Museum*, Vol. I, Part II, London 1912.

BMCat Glass I Harden D. B., *Catalogue of Greek and Roman Glass in The British Museum*, Vol. I, London 1981.

Chamber Tombs Wace A. J. B., *Chamber Tombs at Mycenae*, Archaeologia, Vol. LXXXII, Oxford 1932.

Chronology Furumark A., *The Chronology of Mycenaean Pottery*, Sthlm. 1941.

Conspectus Caskey J. L., "Investigations in Keos, Part II : A Conspectus of the Pottery", *Hesperia* 41, 1972, pp. 357-401.

CVA Brit Walters H. B. and Forsdyke E. J., *CVA*, Great Britain, Fasc. 7 – British Museum Fasc. 5, London 1930.

CVA DK Blinkenberg Chr. and Friis Johansen K., *CVA* Danemark, Fasc. 1 – Copenhague : Musée National Fasc. 1 (Copenhagen 1924). *CVA* Danemark, Fasc. 2 – Copenhague : Musée National Fasc. 2 (Copenhagen 1926).

Deiras Deshayes J., *Argos, Les Fouilles de la Deiras*, Paris 1966 (Études Péloponnésiennes, IV).

Desborough 1964 Desborough V. d'A., *The Last Mycenaeans and their Successors. An Archaeological Survey c. 1200–1000 B.C.* Oxford 1964.

Enkomi IIIa Dikaios P., *Enkomi, Excavations 1948–1958*, Vol. IIIa, Mainz 1969.

French I French E., "Late Helladic IIIA 1 Pottery from Mycenae", *BSA* 59, 1964, p. 241 ff.

French II French E., "Late Helladic IIIA 2 Pottery from Mycenae", *BSA* 60, 1965, p. 159 ff.

French III French E., "A Group of Late Helladic IIIB 1 Pottery from Mycenae", *BSA* 61, 1966, p. 216 ff.

French IV French E., "Pottery from Late Helladic IIIB 1 Destruction Contexts at Mycenae", *BSA* 62, 1967, p. 149 ff.

French V French E., "A Group of Late Helladic IIIB 2 Pottery from Mycenae", *BSA* 64, 1969, p. 71 ff.

French Tarsus French E., "A Reassessement of the Mycenaean Pottery at Tarsus", *AS* XXV, 1975, pp. 53–75.

Gazetteer Hope Simpson R. and Dickinson O. T. P. K., "A Gazetteer of Aegean Civilisation in the Bronze Age, Vol. I : The Mainland and the Islands", *SIMA* Vol. LII, Göteborg 1979.

Ialysos OT Ialysos Old Tombs as published in *CVA* Brit and *BMCat* 1,1.

Ialysos NT Ialysos New Tombs as published in A. Maiuri,*ASAtene* 6–7, 1926 and Jacopi G., *ASAtene* 13–14, 1933.

JRGZM Jahrbuch des Römisch-Germanischen Zentralmuseums Mainz.

Kanta LM III Kanta A., "The Late Minoan III period in Crete. A Survey of Sites, Pottery and Their Distribution", *SIMA* LVIII, Göteborg 1980.

Kition I Karageorghis V., *Excavations at Kition I. The Tombs.* Nicosia 1974.

Lefkandi Popham M. and Milburn E., "Late Helladic IIIC Pottery of Xeropolis (Lefkandi), A Summary", *BSA* 66, 1971, pp. 333–352.

Mee 1982 Mee C., *Rhodes in the Bronze Age*, Warminster 1982.

MP Furumark A., *The Mycenaean Pottery, Analysis and Classification*, Sthlm. 1941.

MPVP Vermeule E. and Karageorghis V., *Mycenaean Pictorial Vase Painting*, Cambridge et al. 1982.

MV Furtwaengler A. and Loeschcke G., *Mykenische Vasen, vorhellenische Thongefässe aus dem Gebiet des Mittelmeeres*, Berlin 1886.

Nouveaux Documents Karageorghis V., *Nouveaux Documents pour l'Étude du Bronze Récent a Chypre, recueil critique et commenté*, (École Française d'Athénes, Études Chypriotes III), Paris 1965.

Perati Iakovidis S. E., "Περατή", Ath. 1970.

Prehistoric Emporio Hood S., *Excavations in Chios 1938–1955, Prehistoric Emporio and Ayio Gala,* Vol. II, Oxford 1982.

Prophitis Elias Rudolf W., "Die Nekropole am Prophitis Elias bei Tiryns", *Tiryns* VI, pp. 23–126. Mainz 197?

Stubbings Levant Stubbings F. H., *Mycenaean Pottery from the Levant,* Cambridge 1951.

Tiryns 1976 Kilian K. et. al., "Ausgrabungen in Tiryns 1976", *AA* 1978, pp. 449–498.

Tiryns 1977 Kilian K. et. al., "Ausgrabungen in Tiryns 1977", *AA* 1979, pp. 379–458.

Tiryns 1978/79 Kilian K. et. al., "Ausgrabungen in Tiryns 1978, 1979", *AA* 1981, pp. 149–256.

Tiryns 1981 Kilian K., "Ausgrabungen in Tiryns 1981", *AA* 1983, pp. 277–328 and Podzuweit Chr., "Bericht zur spätmykenischen Keramik, Ausgrabungen in Tiryns 1981", *AA* 1983, pp. 359–402.

Zygouries Blegen C. W., *Zygouries. A Prehistoric Settlement in the Valley of Cleonae.* Cambridge, Mass. 1928.

18

Introduction

The current state of research on Mycenaean Rhodes was recently summarized by C. Mee in his book on Rhodes in the Bronze Age[5]. A general feature of the sources available for describing the island in Mycenaean times is that they consist almost exclusively of graves and artifacts from graves. It is furthermore significant that excavations when carried out by professional archaeologists, are published in a way which usually affords no possibilities of a detailed examination of burial customs or of the presence of chronological units. Measurements are almost nonexistent in such publications. It should be added that Rhodes is among the areas of the Aegean that have been worst troubled by illegal robber excavations with the result that Rhodian objects are widely scattered in collections in many countries.

Apart from a few poorly published graves excavated by the Italians the graves treated in the present volume are the only contexts known from the southern part of the island, but vast numbers of objects with south Rhodian provenances are found in Museums both on Rhodes and abroad. It should be added that K. F. Kinch's excavations carried out during the earlier years of the century are among the best conducted on the island. As there is no safe testimony for a local Rhodian chronology based on stratigraphy, the general attitude in this work is that a chronological pattern has to be derived from relations with areas of the Mycenaean World where stratigraphical evidence does exist – primarily the Argolid. To this should be added some relative chronological information that can be derived from Kinch's excavations. The problem of relating Rhodian material to material from the surrounding world is no simple one – it is dealt with in some detail in the concluding chapters. Initially it should suffice to note that although Arne Furumark's taxonomy is used to a great extent, an attempt is made to establish more direct stylistic and typological links with more or less well dated material from other areas. It is hardly necessary to emphasize that there is great need of further excavation on the island.

K. F. Kinch's Mycenaean excavations were by-products of the more extensive work carried out at Lindos and Vroulia. The object of the Mycenaean activities was explicitly stated to be the desire to carry out proper excavations of tombs before all were emptied by the peasants and their contents spread worldwide by dealers. The Turkish authorities gave permission to excavate on these grounds too. Nevertheless, as will appear from the following chapters, Kinch usually came too late – in both the Vati area and in the surroundings of Apollakia all the larger cemeteries had been virtually emptied.

A. Catalogue of graves, grave goods and survey materiel

A1 The Vati area

Passia, Vati

The site of Passia was described as follows by Kinch: "Passia is an elevation on the central ridge of Rhodes, at the road to Arnitha. – One hour's walk from Vati and 3/4 of an hour from Arnitha. It consists of white clay "Asprokoma", and slopes towards South at an angle of approximately 10 degrees. Opposite is the larger hill of Palaekastro, towards North the Prophilia is seen. Towards East and West the sea can be seen and in the remote distance above the valley of Apollakia appears the jagged outline of Karphatos. The Passia elevation is covered in pine trees, scrub and heather. The elevation with its southern slope appears from Vati, Arnitha and the valley of Apollakia to be quite a height. The peasants had been excavating the site during the

previous year, having found some not very rich graves.

May 24th, 1904 – The trial-excavation started at Passia where there was hope of finding untouched tombs. Excavation started on the southeastern slope, where the peasants had burnt the heather and scrub in order to find graves. Eight graves had previously been found in the area, but only two of them contained vases".

On July 11th, 1975, the Passia elevation was inspected. The four graves excavated by Kinch were localized S and SW of the hill top on a plateau just below the top (Fig. 2). The pine forest had burnt in 1973 because of a fire which had started in Arnitha. A fire break had been established across the hill. As pointed out by Kinch, the earth is very friable consisting of "aspropilo". Among a few insignificant sherds

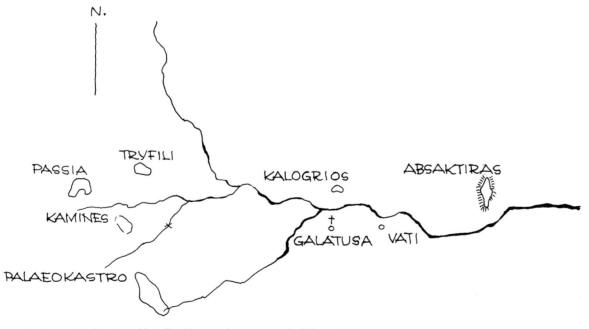

Fig. 1. Sketch of the Vati Area (from Kinch's incomplete manuscript). (M, 1 : 1000).

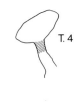
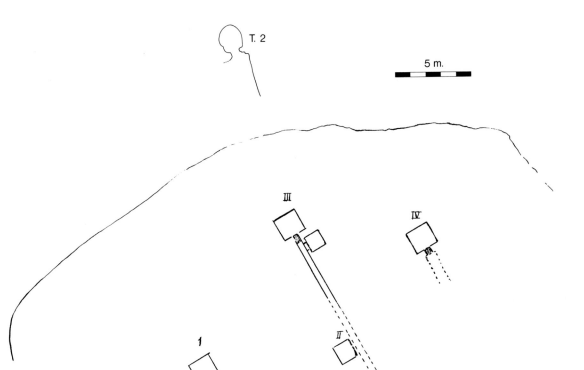

Fig. 2. The cemetery of Passia. Kinch's measurements and the sketch made during the 1975 survey.

M c. 1:400

from the surface collection should be mentioned one rim fragment of a bowl.
No. 1 (Fig. 32) Rim fragment of bowl. Reddish-yellow (7.5 YR 7/6) fabric. Very pale brown (10 YR 8/3), burnished surface.
Estimated diam.: 12 cm.
Dimensions: 3.7 × 7.0 cm.

Passia grave 1

The grave was found one meter below the surface on May 25 1904 (extract from Kinch's description). It was not possible to identify the shape of the dromos, but fragments of decorated and undecorated vases, among them some "from

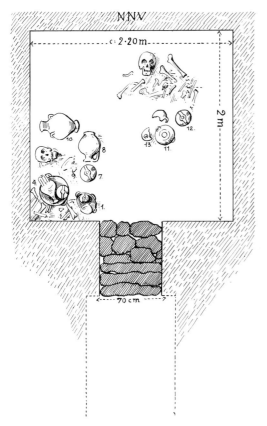

Fig. 3. Drawing of Passia grave 1 (from Kinch's incomplete manuscript).

loosen and clean the vases, many of which were broken because of the pressure of the soil, or the action of roots. Fragments of a few of the broken vases were found outside the stomion – some of the vases had "evidently been deliberately broken" before being placed in larger bowls. It was not possible to make exact measurements of the width and length of the grave – but both seem to have been around 2 metres. The length of the stomion was between 80 and 90 centimetres – other measurements could not be taken.

The vases are noted in the order in which they were excavated (Fig. 3).

One skull was found in the centre at the bottom of the grave. Close to it some bones were found at a slightly higher level. A large number of bones (animal bones?) and two skulls with as many bones as could be supposed to belong to two bodies lay in the southwestern corner. "Thus the bodies were not placed in the graves in the same way as, for instance, they were at Apsaktiras – regularly with the heads towards N and the legs towards the entrance at the south side". Most of the vases were found in the SW corner – a few in the centre. During the 1975 survey neither dromos nor dimensions of chamber could be identified.

Sherds from the dromos (Fig. 4). The sherds depicted are all from Kinch's manuscript – a short description was also given in his sketchbook (not one of these sherds has been identified in Copenhagen or in Istanbul).

a.-b. – from the same pot. Red fabric. Yellowish slip. Red paint.
a : 8.5 × 6.0 cm.
b : 8.0 × 3.0 cm.

a Bucchero vase with handle" were found in front of the door. The stomion was constructed of stones laid vertically towards the entrance and of stones laid horizontally towards the chamber. The roof had collapsed and the grave was excavated from above. In the chamber solid clay was found everywhere and it proved very difficult to

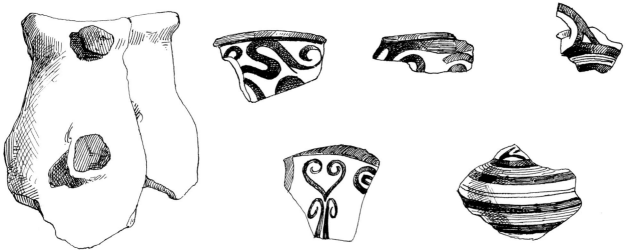

Fig. 4. Sherds from dromos, Passia grave 1 (from Kinch's incomplete manuscript). 1 : 3.

Fig. 5. Bowl 1,1, (Ist. inv. no. 4265) from Passia grave 1. Photo and drawing by Helvig Kinch. 1 : 2.

c. –   tile-red fabric. Black paint.
         : 4.5 × 6.0 cm.
d. –   black fabric.
         : 16 × 18 cm.
e. –   pink fabric. Red paint.
         : 7.5 × 7.0 cm.
f. –   pinkish fabric. Decoration in brownish-
         red altering to very dark paint.
         : 10.5 × 9.0 cm.

Catalogue of grave goods

1,1 (Ist. inv.no. 4265) (Fig. 5, Fig. 120). Shallow, angular bowl with a low conical ring-foot and two opposed handles with circular section on the rim, which is thickened and slopes inwards. The bowl was found in six pieces. Repaired at the foot and on the body with gypsum. Grey fabric. The outer surface covered with light yellow slip – the inside with darker yellow slip. There is light yellow slip under the bottom. Decoration in yellow-brown paint partly altered to black. The upper part is decorated with parallel chevrons (FM 58,34) between horizontal bands. There is a triangle pattern (FM 61A,1) in the handle zone. The handles are decorated with cross-striped paint. The lower part of the body is decorated with horizontal zones of lines, and there are horizontal bands on the foot.
Max. H. : 15.1 cm (over the highest handle).

Max. W. : 25.1 cm (from one handle to the other).
The stirrup jar no. 1,2 and the kylix no. 1,3 were found inside bowl 1,1.

1,2 (Ist. inv.no. 4261) (Fig. 6, Fig. 116). Globular stirrup jar (FS 176) on a low ring base, slightly forward-sloping, splaying spout. Preserved totally intact. Red-brown fabric. The surface (except under the bottom) is covered by a fat yellow, slightly reddish slip. Paint in alternating brownish/black, rather matt colours in horizontal zones from bottom to handle zone. In the uppermost free zone on the body – below the handle zone – decoration in groups with zig-zag (FM 61,3) and quirk (FM 48,5). A decoration of five joining semicircles in a triangular patch (FM 42,21) in the handle zone. The oval bands round the spout and the top are connected, thus forming a figure of eight. Three concentric circles are seen on the top plate. The sides of the strap handles are painted.
Max. H. : 13.9 cm.
Max. W. : 12.5 cm.

24

Fig. 6. Stirrup jar 1,2 (Ist. inv. no. 4261) from Passia grave 1. Seen from the side and from above. 1 : 2.

1,3 (Ist. inv.no. 4256) (Fig. 7, Fig. 121). Kylix with rounded bowl and low stem (FS 257). The base is hollowed out underneath. Composed of 12 sherds; a few pieces are lacking. Reddish-brown fabric. Light yellow slip. Reddish-brown lustrous paint. Stem and base decorated with bands. Paint on the upper side of the strap handles and a band on the inside and outside of the rim. The zones between the handles are decorated with space-filling cuttlefish having six arms (FM 21 closest to no. 7) on both sides. Added white lines on the arms and on the body. The cuttlefish crosses the uppermost band on the stem and the band on the rim.
Max. H. : 17.1 cm.
Max. diam. of rim : 15.9 cm.
Diam. at handles : 23.3 cm

Fig. 7. Kylix 1,3 (Ist. inv. no. 4256) from Passia grave 1. 1 : 2.

25

Fig. 8. Krater 1,4 (Ist. inv. no. 4246) from Passia grave 1. 1 : 2.

1,4 (Ist. inv.no. 4246) (Fig. 8, Fig. 119). Large open krater with two horizontal handles and shallow ring-base (FS 281). Almost complete. Reddish fabric. Surface covered with a faint, light yellow slip; the surface appears reddish-yellow where uncovered by slip. Decoration in lustrous black paint. A band on the base, three bands under the handles, a band below the rim, the rim itself being painted inside and out. The handles, of circular section, have a painted band which continues below them, thus cutting the horizontal bands round the belly. Wavy line pattern (FM 53) in the handle zone.
Max. H. : 22.5 cm.
Max. W. : 26.3
The piriform jug no. *1,5* and the stirrup jar *1,6* were found inside the krater *1,4*.

1,5 (Ist. inv.no. 4247) (Fig. 9, Fig. 118). Piriform jug with high spout and three grooved strap-handles with raised edge (FS 151). Low ring-base. Raised collar at the base of the spout. The spout is broken and a few sherds are missing on shoulder and belly. Yellowish fabric. Thin yellow slip. Decoration in lustrous black paint altering to reddish-brown. Horizontal bands and lines on body and foot. Five flowers of Furumark's III A : 2 types (FM 18) are seen in the handle zone.
Max. H. : 25.5 cm.
Max. D. : 16.5 cm.
Published: *Arkæologens Rhodos*, Fig. 16.

1,6 (Ist. inv.no. 4270) (Fig. 10, Fig. 116). Miniature squat, globular, stirrup jar with ring-base (FS 171). Pierced bottom. Reddish fabric. Brownish, rich slip. Decoration in brown, rather matt paint. Horizontal bands and lines round the body, oval band connects spout and neck. The top plate decorated with a spiral. The upper part of the body is decorated with four circular "sea-anemone" motifs (FM 27).
Max. H. : 6.8 cm.
Max. W. : 6.3 cm.

1,7 (Ist. inv.no. 4259) (Fig. 11, Fig. 116). Stirrup jar of carinated squat, globular shape (FS 180) with ring-base. Restored at one handle and at

Fig. 9. Piriform jug 1,5 (Ist. inv.no. 4247) from Passia grave 1. 1 : 2. Photo and drawing by H. Kinch.

Fig. 10. Stirrup jar 1,6 (Ist. inv.no. 4270) from Passia grave 1. Seen from the side and from above. 1 : 1.

Fig. 11. Stirrup jar 1,7 (Ist. inv.no. 4259) from Passia grave 1. Seen from the side and from above. 1 : 2.

spout. Reddish-yellow, thin slip (peeled). Body decoration of varying red and brown paint in horizontal zones consisting of broad bands and thin lines. In the handle/spout zone, decoration of joining semicircles (FM 42), partly as "triangular patch" (FM 42,33), partly (on the opposite side of the spout) as a "space-filling net" (FM 42,19). Spout and neck connected by a band. The mouth of the spout is painted. The top plate decorated with a spiral having a dot in the centre, the strap-handles are decorated along the edge and at the root – thus forming a U-shaped pattern.

Max. H. : 13.7 cm.
Max. W. : 17.3 cm.

1,8 (Ist. inv.no. 4257) (Fig. 12, Fig. 118). Jug with cut-away spout. (The spout is reconstructed – probably incorrectly – see also p. 98). Globular body. Small ring-foot, slightly concave bottom (FS 148). There is a bead at the transition between spout and body. The spout is broken, but repaired with gypsum. Red, fine-grained fabric with a few larger grains seen on the surface, which is covered by a rich, light yellow slip. Lustrous brown/reddish-brown

Fig. 12. Jug 1,8 (Ist. inv.no. 4257) from Passia grave 1. Left and right side 1 : 4.

Fig. 13. Undecorated kylix 1,9 (Ist. inv.no. 4254) from Passia grave 1. 1 : 2.

painted decoration. Groups of horizontal, parallel bands around the belly. The decoration in the handle zone consists of vertical, parallel zig-zag lines, one triangle motif (FM 61A,1) (with four congruous triangles) and a flower pattern (FM 18 – local variant) to the right of the handle. A band connects the spout and the handle. Three horizontal bands around the spout – the lowest on the bead. Two filled triangles (FM 61A,3) at each side of the spout in the uppermost zone. The handle has a circular section, with cross-lines on the upper side. Two broad vertical lines of paint run from the handle zone down on the upper part of the belly. A few wheel traces on the bottom.
Max. H. : 25.8 cm.
Max. W. : 20.5 cm.

1,9 (Ist. inv.no. 4254) (Fig. 13, Fig. 121) High-stemmed kylix with two handles. Carinated cup. Restored with gypsum at the rim and on the body. Fabric grey with a red tinge. Surface colour yellowish-grey with faint traces of a thin yellow slip. The inside of the cup is "corrugated" as a result of turning on a wheel.
Max. H. : 18.0 cm (rim).
Max. H. : 18.4 cm (highest handle).
Max. W. : 17.5 cm (rim).
Max. W. : 24.2 cm (including handles).

1,10 (Ist. inv.no. 4242) (Fig. 14, Fig. 117).

Ovoid-biconical jar with cylindrical neck and three vertical strap-handles (FS 37–38). Ring base. One handle restored with gypsum. Restored in a number of places on the body. The surface is covered by a dark yellow, thin slip – rather peeled off. Lustrous paint in varying yellow-brownish colours. Groups of parallel lines on the body. Parallel, vertical zig-zag pattern in the handle zone. The same paint is used for the neck both inside and out. Parallel cross-lines on the upper side of the handles.
Max. H. : 42.0 cm.
Max. W. : 33.7 cm.

1,11 (Ist. inv.no. 4266) (Fig. 15, Fig. 121). Deep bowl with curved section, two opposed horizontal handles and ring foot (FS 285). The bowl is repaired with gypsum in four places. The fabric is greyish with a red tinge. The surface covered with a dark yellow slip. Decoration in black, lustrous paint – partly altered to brown. Brownish paint on the foot. A broad band under the handle zone. A decoration of antithetic spirals (FM 50,4) in the handle zone, at both sides. The handles are painted on the upper side and at the root. The inside of the bowl is painted black except for a circular, central section left unpainted. Traces of turning on a rather fast wheel.
Max. H. : 12.5 cm.
Max. W. : 18.6 cm.

Fig. 14. Ovoid biconical jar 1,10
(Ist. inv.no. 4242) from Passia grave 1.
1 : 4.

1,12 (Ist. inv.no. 4249) (Fig. 16, Fig. 116). Depressed globular (perked-up) stirrup jar with ring base (FS 176). Somewhat restored. One side of the spout is missing. Reddish fabric. The surface covered with a brownish-yellow slip. Deco-

ration in matt brown altering to black. Horizontal bands decorate the ring-base and belly. The two uppermost zones below the handle zone are decorated with parallel chevrons (FM 58,32) (the uppermost zone), and vertical, parallel lines

Fig. 15. Deep bowl 1,11
(Ist. inv.no. 4266)
from Passia grave 1. 1 : 2.

30

Fig. 16. Stirrup jar 1,12 (Ist. inv.no. 4249) from Passia grave 1. Seen from the side and from above. 1 : 2.

in groups. The handle zone is decorated with spirals: a single spiral (FM 51:15) and a leaf (?) at each side of the spout. Opposite the spout is an antithetic stemmed spiral pattern (FM 51 – see fig. 16). Another spiral decorates the top plate. The edges of the strap-handles are painted and the mouth of the spout has a band. The spout and the neck are connected by an oval band. Wheel traces under the bottom.
Max. H. : 18.5 cm.
Max. W. : 15.9 cm.

1,13 (not found in Istanbul) (Fig. 17). Description according to Kinch: Small stirrup jar, H : 0.12 m. Width at belly : 0,097 m light clay, no slip. Dark brown, lustrous paint. Horizontal bands. Three triangular patterns in the handle zone. Spiral pattern on the top plate. Part of spout missing.

Passia grave 2

(Fig. 18, Fig. 19). From Kinch's incomplete manuscript (extract): The roof had collapsed and the grave was excavated from above. There were two large and some smaller stones at the bottom of the grave (along the northern side). Most likely the bodies had been placed by or near the stones. One of the large, somewhat irregular stones measured 60 × 50 cm, thickness

20 cm. "In the cemetery of Apsaktiras, for instance in grave II, similar stones were found". Neither dromos nor stomion could be found – but it seems as if the entrance was connected with the dromos of another grave. A skull was found on the stone slabs in the NW corner together with a small stirrup jar. Not far off lay a sword (No. 5) in three pieces and bones, evidently constituting an entire leg. Close by was a well preserved skull and other bones. In the south western part of the grave were two skulls

Fig. 17. Stirrup jar 1,13 from Passia grave 1. Approximately 1 : 2 (from an old photo).

31

Fig. 18. Passia grave 2 from the South. The depression in the background is of recent origin (July 1975).

lying so close to each other that they were picked up together. Some minor vases, mainly broken, were placed close by (2–4). Furthermore one silver ring, an arrow head and a bronze ring were found close to the sword (actually six skulls are seen on the drawing, Fig. 19).

During the 1975 survey the eastern part of the dromos seemed recognizable but the western side had been cut away. The height of the stomion was 1.20 m on the eastern side. The chamber was evidently oval even if the dimensions could

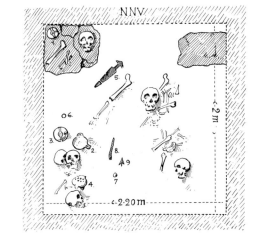

Fig. 19. Passia grave 2. (Sketch from Kinch's incomplete manuscript).

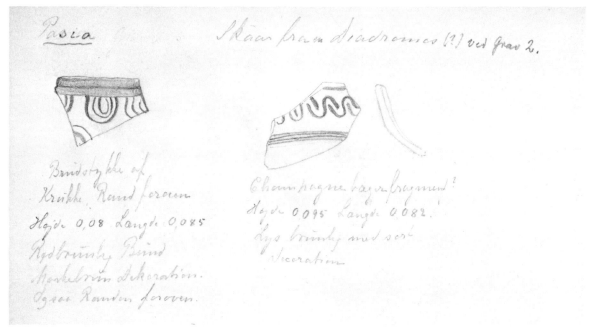

Fig. 20. Two sherds from the dromos of Passia grave 2 (from Kinch's sketchbook).

not be established in detail because of the fallen stones.

Sherds from dromos (Fig. 20). The two sherds depicted are from Kinch's sketchbook – no sherds were identified in Copenhagen or in Istanbul. Kinch gives the following brief descriptions:

a. – rim sherd from jar. Reddish-brown fabric. Dark brown paint – even on top of rim.
H : 8 cm.
L : 8.5 cm.
b. – fragment of champagne cup (?). Light yellowish fabric.
Black decoration.
H : 9.5 cm.
L : 8.2 cm.

Catalogue of grave goods

2,1 (Ist. inv.no. 4263) (Fig. 21, Fig. 116). Squat globular (weighed-down) stirrup jar with ring-foot (FS 171). Part of the spout missing but otherwise complete. Horizontal bands around the belly and at the ring-foot. Two vertical bars in the upper zone (below the handle zone). Reddish fabric. Reddish-brown slip. Reddish-brown paint altering to black-brown. A decoration of parallel chevrons (FM 58) in the handle zone. Dots and U-shaped patterns at the root of the handles. A spiral on the top plate, paint on top of the strap-handles. Band on top of the spout. A band connects the spout and neck.
Max. H. : 10.6 cm.
Max. W. : 9.3 cm.

Fig. 21. Stirrup jar 2,1 (Ist. inv.no. 4263) from Passia grave 2. Seen from the side and from above. 1 : 2.

Fig. 22. Cup with bridge-spout 2,2 (Ist. inv.no. 4269) from Passia grave 2. 1 : 2.

2,2 (Ist. inv.no. 4269) (Fig. 22, Fig. 120). Semi-globular cup with bridge-spout (F 249). The spout is not opposite the handle but at an angle of around 120°. Parts of the body and part of the horizontal band are restored. Reddish-brown fabric, no slip. Decoration in a brown, peeling, lustrous paint changing into red. The rim was originally covered with a band – now marked by a faint sketching. Inside, the colour goes down to 2.5 cm from the rim. The outside of the strap-handle is painted. A band runs around the bowl just beneath the handle. The handle/spout zone is decorated with a zigzag (FM 61) or wavy line intersected by handle and spout. The foot is coloured.
Max. H. : 8.1 cm.
Diam. : 11.0 cm.
Diam. (handle incl.) : 13.1 cm.
Diam. (spout incl.) : 13.9 cm.

2,3 (Ist. inv.no. 4264) (Fig. 23, Fig. 116). Globu-

lar stirrup jar with ring-foot (FS 176). Rather poorly preserved – parts of the body filled with gypsum. Grey fabric. Surface covered with a thin (peeled) yellow slip. Decorated in matt red/black paint (different firing conditions). Horizontal bands around the body – thinner parallel lines between broader bands. The uppermost zone below the handle zone is filled with cross-hatch pattern (diaper net : FM 57:2). Decoration of flower motifs in the handle zone (FM 18). The paint on the top plate and on top of the strap-handles is almost totally peeled off. An oval band connects the spout and the neck.
Max. H. : 12.1 cm.
Max. W. : 11.0 cm.

2,4 (Ist. inv.no. 4464) (Fig. 24). Incense burner or brazier (thymiaterion) with holes, rows of knobs and three feet (FS 316). The upper part is missing and two feet are broken. Grey fabric and surface. Handmade.
Wall thickness : 0.5 cm.
Max. H. (pres.) : 6.4 cm.
Max. W. (pres.) : 8.6 cm.

2,5 (Copenh. inv.no. 12412) (Fig. 25). A short sword with T-flanged pommel. The grip has raised edges. The sword is almost intact, only lacking a triangular piece of the blade. Below the pommel are two U-shaped concavities which, through two edged beads, run into the grip with parallel sides. The transition to the blade is marked by two square shoulders. There is a horizontal burr across the blade at the lower termination of the shoulder-part. This border thus marks the lower limit to the extent of the original covering of organic material (bone or ivory). At the side of the grip (where the edges are parallel) and at the top of the pommel is a

Fig. 23. Stirrup jar 2,3 (Ist. inv.no. 4264) from Passia grave 2. Seen from the side and from above. 1 : 2.

Fig. 24. Thymiaterion 2,4 (Ist. inv.no. 4464) from Passia grave 2. Drawing by Helvig Kinch. 1 : 2.

faint notch (W : 0.5 cm) along the centreline. The three nails in the flange are preserved, but the uppermost one is broken. The blade is flat and slightly curved.
Max. L. : 39.0 cm.
Raised sides of the grip : H. : 1.8 cm.
W. pommel : 7.0 cm.
Rivet L. : 2.3 cm.
Published: *Arkæologens Rhodos*, Fig. 22.

2,6 (Copenh. inv.no. 12408) (Fig. 26). Silver finger-ring with an oval bezel terminating centrally in a point. Ribbonshaped ring.
Oval sheet : 2.2 × 1.6 cm.
Diam. ring (inner) : 1.8 cm.
Ribbon W. : 0.5 cm.

2,7 (Copenh. inv.no. 12380) (Fig. 27). Ribbon-shaped finger ring in bronze.
Diam. (inner) : 1.6 cm.
Ribbon W. : 0.6 cm.

2,8 (Copenh. inv.no. 12415) (Fig. 28). One-edged bronze knife. Probably intact. The termination of the short flanged grip is slightly convex. One rivet hole (diam. : 0.25 cm) and two rivets (L. : 0.8 cm) in the flange. Parts of a pale yellow organic covering – probably ivory – are preserved on both sides of the flange. The blade is rather flat and slightly curved. The back is thickened.
L. : 13.8 cm.
Max. W. : 1.3 cm.
W. of back : 0.45 cm.
Grip L. : 2.8 cm.

2,9 (Copenh. inv.no. 12381) (Fig. 29) Bronze arrowhead. The blade is assymmetrical – one side is straight, the other convex. The straight one is broken at the bottom. The convex side terminates at the foot in a faint hook. The mid part of the blade is thickened, this thickening continuing in the upper part of the point which, at the bottom, tends to be slimmer with a pointed oval section.
L. : 5.1 cm.

Fig. 25. Short sword 2,5 (Copenhagen inv.no. 12412) from Passia grave 2. Slightly reconstructed drawing by Helvig Kinch, and a photo. Drawing : 1 :2, photo : 1 : 4.

Passia grave 3

(Fig. 30, Fig. 31). According to Kinch, grave 3 contained nothing, but as a dromos was visible and a chamber was detected it was presumed to be a grave. Furthermore it had to be recalled that the epistat stated: "Of the eight graves pre-

Fig. 26. Silver finger-ring 2,6 (Copenhagen inv.no 12408) from Passia grave 2. Drawing by Helvig Kinch, and a photo. 1 : 1.

Fig. 27. Finger-ring in bronze 2,7 (Copenhagen inv.no. 12380) from Passia grave 2. Drawing by Helvig Kinch. 1 : 1.

viously found by the peasants at Passia, only two contained anything''. In the eastern wall of the dromos, around 1 m from the entrance of grave 3, there was a large stone (H : c. 60 cm, W : 65 cm). According to Kinch, this stone repaired a hole resulting from damage to the wall of an older grave when the dromos for grave 3 was dug. This older chamber towards the east had been opened and robbed at an earlier date.

During the 1975 survey the roof of the chamber was found to have collapsed. The dromos was quite well preserved. The side chamber (on the east) was found to be connected with the dromos, not separated from it as on Kinch's drawing. As can be seen from Fig. 2, the chamber was rather irregular.

Fig. 28. One-edged knife 2,8 (Copenhagen inv.no. 12415) from Passia grave 2. Drawing by Helvig Kinch. 1 : 2.

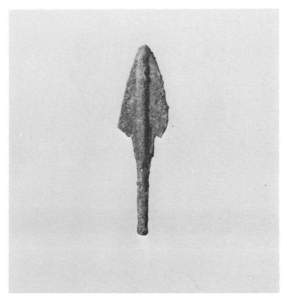

Fig. 29. Bronze arrowhead 2,9 (Copenhagen inv.no. 12381) from Passia grave 2. 1 : 1.

Sherds from the dromos. During the 1975 survey the following sherds were collected from grave 3:

– Bottom sherd with ring-base, open-shaped jar. Reddish-brown fabric. Brown monochrome on outside (Fig. 32).

– One wall fragment of a brown monochrome vessel painted inside and out – probably a LHIII A2 kylix.

Passia grave 4

(Fig. 33, Fig. 34). Description from Kinch's incomplete manuscript: The grave was excavated on May 28th, 1904. It is located further east than the others. The stomion was filled with many stones, one of which measured : 97 × 46 × 14 cm. Towards the dromos two stones were placed on end, while towards the chamber they lay horizontally in courses. All stones were of asproporos. A few, small pieces of charcoal were found in front of the door. The stomion had the following dimensions : W : c. 70 cm, H : 1.11 m, L : 1.07 m. Close to the door was found a large jar (No. 1) with the mouth facing the entrance. Next to this was the jug No. 2 (ref. Fig. 34). The right side of the grave was filled with bones and skulls, comprising a total of four bodies. The bones were in a jumble and two skulls faced the northern inner wall. Kinch suggests that the bodies were originally buried in another grave and later removed to grave 4. A small jug (No. 13) was found next to the skulls, as also an idol (No. 14) and the beads No. 15.

36

Fig. 30. Passia grave 3, dromos and chamber from the South. (July 1975).

The 1975 survey reported that the roof in the chamber had collapsed, while the roof of the stomion was still preserved. The dromos was in good condition with sloping sides (narrower at the top than at the bottom).

Sherds from the dromos (Fig. 35). Three sherds were found in the dromos and depicted by Kinch. None of them has been identified in Istanbul or in Copenhagen, but Kinch gave the following short description in his sketchbook:

a. – side fragment of a bottle. Yellow surface, brownish rings, framed by black lines.
  Dimensions : 20 × 16.5 cm.

b. – sherd with red decoration on a yellow surface.
  Dimensions : 10 × 8 cm.
c. – base, stem and lower part of bowl of an undecorated kylix.
  Brownish surface.
  Diameter of base : 6.5 cm.
  H : 7.5 cm.

Catalogue of grave goods

4,1 (Ist. inv.no. 4240?) (Fig. 36). This jar was not described and no drawing was made in Istanbul. K. F. Kinch gives the following description:

37

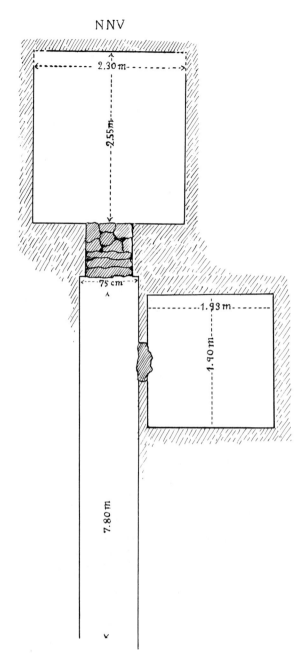

Fig. 31. Passia grave 3 with side chamber. (From Kinch's incomplete manuscript).

Fig. 33. Passia grave 4. Dromos, entrance and chamber from the South. (July 1975).

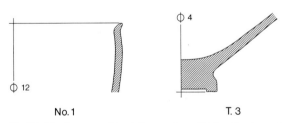

Fig. 32. Rim fragment of bowl from surface collection, Passia no. 1 and sherd from dromos in Passia grave 3.

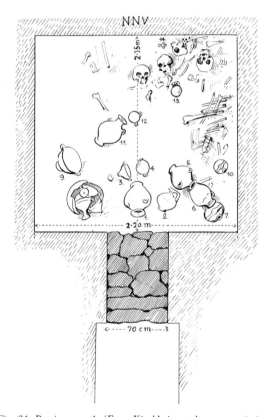

Fig. 34. Passia grave 4. (From Kinch's incomplete manuscript).

Fig. 35. Three sherds from the dromos of Passia grave 4 (from Kinch's sketchbook).

"Large jar with foot and three small, vertical handles. One handle missing, as well as part of the foot disk and part of the collar (FS 35/FM 70).
H. : 4 cm.
W. at belly : 35.6 cm.
D. of collar : 15.3 cm.
D. of mouth : 12 cm.
Yellowish fabric. No slip. The lustrous paint is dark brown/black, red in one area on the shoul-

der. The foot is painted black with a ring above. Higher up, three rings encircle the belly, and further up again there are three rings below the shoulder. The shoulder is decorated with scale patterns having a tongue in each scale interrupted by the handles, which are dark and surrounded by a ring. Narrow rings just below the neck. The neck is black with cross-lines at the collar. Lustrous paint on the inner part of the mouth. The vase smells aromatic inside".

4,2 (Ist. inv.no. 4248) (Fig. 37, Frontspiece 1 and Fig. 118). Globular, conical jug (FS 120) with one handle and horizontal mouth. Restored with gypsum at neck and handle. Red fabric. Surface covered with a thin, pale yellow slip – changing to red in places. A horizontal band runs around the piece just above the bottom, which is slightly concave. Two parallel, horizontal bands encircle the centre of the belly. The zone between the uppermost band and the neck is decorated with two bird pictures, one at each side of the handle. The feet and the tip of the tails continue into the

Fig. 36. Jar 4,1 (Ist. inv.no. 4240 ?) from Passia grave 4. 1 : 4.

Fig. 37. Jug 4,2 (Ist. inv.no. 4248)
from Passia grave 4. Photo of one
side, and detail of one of the birds
(Helvig Kinch). 1 : 2.

uppermost band. The bodies of the birds are decorated with isolated spirals, isolated semicircles (FM 43) and parallel curved lines at the neck. At the handle are three ring-shaped figures. Painted bands at the root of the spout, just above the the centre of the spout, and at the slightly thickened rim (extending down the in-

side). The strap-handle is painted on the outside. No slip at the bottom. No wheel traces.
Max. H. : 22.7 cm.
Max. W. : 19.9 cm.
Published : *Arkæologens Rhodos*, Fig. 17. *Nationalmuseets Arbejdsmark* 1976, Figs. 3 and 5.

Fig. 38. Deep bowl 4,3
(Ist. inv.no. 4267) from
Passia grave 4. 1 : 2.

40

Fig. 39. Kylix 4,4
(Ist. inv.no. 4255) from
Passia grave 4. 1 : 2.

4,3 (Ist. inv.no. 4267) (Fig. 38, Fig. 121). Deep bowl with a low ring-foot (FS 284). Some restoration on the bowl. Red fabric. Surface covered in a yellow slip with a reddish tinge. Matt varying brown/black paint. A band encircles the low foot. The handle zone, which is delimited downwards by a horizontal band below the handles, is decorated with two antithetic spiral patterns having a central triglyph (FM 50) that are rather sloppily executed. The painted handles have a circular section. The paint continues across the horizontal band. A band on the outside and the inside of the rim. Wheel traces on the inside of the bowl and at the bottom.
Max. H. : 11.3 cm.
Max. W. (across the handles) : 20.5 cm.

4,4 (Ist. inv.no. 4255) (Fig. 39, Fig. 121). High-stemmed kylix. Parts of stem and foot restored. Reddish-brown fabric. The surface is covered by a reddish-yellow, rather rich slip. Decoration in a red/brown "matt" paint (rich, but not lustrous) altering to black/brown. The disc foot has three encircling bands, the stem four. There are three narrow, parallel rings at the transition between bowl and stem. In the handle zone are two antithetic spirals (FM 50) whose stems are con-

nected by a pattern of concentric arches (7 on one side, 6 on the other). The rim and the upper side of the simple strap-handles are painted. Wheel traces under the disc foot and on inner and outer sides of the bowl.
Max. H. : 20.4 cm.
Max. W. (bowl): 16.4–16.8 cm.
Max W. (including handles) : 22.8 cm.

4,5 (Ist. inv.no. 4243) (Fig. 40, Frontispiece 2 and Fig. 117) Jar of heavy piriform – ovoid shape, with a high, incurved, cylindrical neck and three vertical strap-handles with a central raised bead (FS 37). Part of foot missing, otherwise complete. Reddish/brown very hard fabric. The surface is covered with a fine washed, light, bright yellow slip. The lustrous paint is reddish/brown altering in places to black/brown. The paint on the foot extends up on to the lower part of the body; there is an encircling band slightly higher up. Three broad bands encircle the central part of the belly. The handle zone above these three bands is decorated with three different types of vertical, panelled decoration – separated by the handles. Each picture plane comprises decoration in five vertical panels :
Zone 1) shows a scale pattern (FM 70,1) in

41

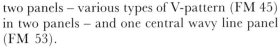

Fig. 40. Jar 4,5 (Ist. inv.no. 4243) from Passia grave 4. Seen from the side and from above, and one detailed drawing of panel (Helvig Kinch). 1 : 4.

two panels – various types of V-pattern (FM 45) in two panels – and one central wavy line panel (FM 53).

Zone 2) all panels are decorated with bivalve shell chains (FM 25) – in one panel the shells are bounded by vertical wavy lines.

Zone 3) one panel showing bivalve shells – three panels showing a rather specific, vertical "joining-U" pattern – and one panel with cross-hatched pattern, diaper net (FM 57). Vertical, parallel wavy lines border one side of the picture plane. Hanging concentric arches encircle the foot of the monochrome neck. Quirk patterns (FM 48,6) separated by groups of parallel lines are found on top of the collar – a band of depth around 1.5 cm is painted inside. The upper side of the handles is painted – but downwards the paint divides into two bands crossing the uppermost of the three central bands. Wheel traces.
Max. H. : 33.8 cm.
Max. W. : 26.2 cm.

4,6 (Ist. inv.no. 4239?) (Fig. 41, Fig. 117). Large ovoid jar with a low cylindrical collar neck (with incurved sides) and two vertical handles with circular section. Some restoration. Red/brown fabric. The surface is covered by a fine light yellow slip – changing into red in places. Decora-

Fig. 41. Jar 4,6 (Ist. inv.no. 4239 ?) from Passia grave 4. 1 : 4.

42

Fig. 42. Stirrup jar 4,7 (Ist. inv.no. 4258) from Passia grave 4. Seen from the side and from above. 1 : 2.

tion in a red ochre colour (partly lustrous) changing into black in places. The paint is rather peeled. Horizontal, encircling bands on the belly. The foot is painted; above the foot, a line and a band – two bands on the lower part of the belly – three broad bands below the handles. A wavy-line pattern consisting of one broad band and one line in the handle zone. The neck is

painted inside and out. Wheel traces at the bottom.
Max. H. : 41.3 cm.
Max. W. : 32.9 cm.

4,7 (Ist. inv.no. 4258) (Fig. 42, Fig. 116). Conical stirrup jar with a rather pronounced torus disc base (FS 182). The walls are extremely thin –

Fig. 43. Stemmed krater 4,8 (Ist. inv.no. 4244) from Passia grave 4. Photo of front panel, and detailed drawing of reverse. (by Helvig Kinch). 1 : 4.

Fig. 44. Four unpainted kylikes 4,8, a-d (Ist. inv.no. 4250–4253) from Passia grave 4. 1 : 2.

e.g. just 0.2 cm on the belly. Put together from many pieces – only few are missing. The fabric is grey with a faint reddish tinge. The surface is covered by a fine washed, thick, light yellow slip. Bright red lustrous paint changing to brown in a few places. The foot is painted, except for the lowest vertical part that is only slipped. The zone between the foot and the next broad band is filled by 6–7 very fine, parallel, encircling lines. The same type of delicate line is seen between the next band and the band just below the carination, while the carination zone is filled by N-patterns (FM 60,2). The three last zones below the handle zone contain a circumcurrent quirk pattern (FM 48,12) enclosed by two zones with fine lines. The handle zone is decorated with varying parallel chevrons (FM 58) and trefoil rockwork (FM 9,23). There is a ring at the root of the spout and the false neck (no connection). The strap-handles are painted on the upper side and the top disc shows a pattern of concentric circles (FM 41) (six concentric circles around a central dot). The circles are undoubtedly drawn by means of a compass. A ring encircles the mouth of the spout.

Max. H. : 16.1 cm.
Max. W. (on belly) : 18.4 cm.
Published : *Arkæologens Rhodos*, Fig. 18.

4,8 (Ist. inv.no. 4244) (Fig. 43, Fig. 119). Stemmed krater (FS 9) with vertical strap-handles. Somewhat restored. Red-brown fabric. The surface is covered by a rather thin reddish-yellow slip. Decoration in reddish-brown paint. The foot and part of the stem are painted, and there is a band slightly higher up. Bands encircle the bowl just below the handles. The handle zone is furnished with two different, panelled friezes. The motifs are seemingly very local variations of Mycenaean III flowers (FM 18). On one side (the front) the central panel with bivalve shells (FM 25) is enclosed by double lines – the panel ends upwards in a volute (very like FM 18,25). Above the volute are three oval cross-hatched figures (comp. FM 18,52–53) enclosed by two U-shaped patterns. Above this (under the rim) is a wavy-line pattern. The vertical zone between the central pattern and the next two flower panels with vertical wavy-lines is filled by two U-shaped figures – with a spiral in the one and a strange cross-hatched figure in the other (it looks almost like a bagpipe or a stylized bird).

One of the flower patterns has a central filling pattern with bivalve shells, the other a vertical wavy line. The other side (rear) has likewise five Myc. III flower panels – with bivalve shells and

one with a wavy line – separated by five lozenge patterns (FM 73,14). A U-shaped figure encloses one of the handles. The rim and the upper side of the handles (partly restored) are painted. Wheel traces.
Max. H. : 32.0 cm.
Max. W. (at the rim) : 33.8 cm.
Inside the stemmed krater 4,8 were found the four almost identical high-stemmed kylikes : 4,8,a – 4,8,b – 4,8,c – 4,8,d.

4,8,a (Ist. inv.no. 4250) (Fig. 44, Fig. 121). High-stemmed kylix with two vertical strap-handles. A sherd is missing from the rim. Red fabric. Reddish-yellow, burnished slip. Clear wheel traces (washboard surface) on the inside of the bowl.
Max. H. : 18.6 cm.
Max. W. (across the handles) : 22.0 cm.

4,8,b (Ist. inv.no. 4251) (Fig. 44, Fig. 121). High-stemmed kylix with two vertical strap-handles. The fabric is a fairly light reddish-brown in colour. Reddish-yellow, burnished slip on the surface. A darker colouring on the stem might be the result of a repair in antiquity. Washboard surface on the inner side of the bowl.
Max. H. : 18.6 cm.
Max. W. (across handles) : 22.0 cm.

4,8,c (Ist. inv.no. 4252) (Fig. 44, Fig. 121). High-stemmed kylix with two vertical strap-handles. Well preserved. Red fabric. The surface is covered with a red-yellow burnished slip. Wheel traces are seen clearly at the stem and inside the bowl.
Max. H. : 20.4 cm.
Max. W. (across handles) : 24.5 cm.

4,8,d (Ist. inv.no. 4253) (Fig. 44, Fig. 121). High-stemmed kylix with two vertical strap-handles. The stem has been broken, otherwise the piece is well preserved. Red fabric. The surface is covered with a red-yellow slip – slightly burnished.
Max. H. : 18.5 cm.
Max. W. (across handles) : 23.0 cm.

4,9 (Ist. inv.no. 4245?) (Fig. 45, Fig. 119). Large bell krater with horizontal handles of circular section. Small ring-foot (FS 282). Several side fragments are missing. Red fabric. The surface is covered by a burnished, red-yellow slip. Decoration in a black-brown rather matt paint (much peeled off). Bands encircle the ring-foot and a further two are found above the foot. Three encircling rings below and above the handle zone. Decorated with a zigzag pattern, consisting of parallel lines interrupted by simple flower patterns, in the handle zone. The rim is painted

Fig. 45. Bell krater 4,9
(Ist. inv.no. 4245 ?)
from Passia grave 4. 1 : 4.

inside and out, the handles on the outside. Clear wheel traces.

Max. H. : 28.5 cm.

Max. W. (across handles) : 40.0 cm.

4,10 (Ist. inv.no. 4260) (Fig. 46, Fig. 116). Depressed globular (somewhat perked-up) stirrup jar (FS 173) preserved totally intact. Red fabric. Surface covered by a red-yellow slip. Decoration in matt red-brown paint – where the paint is thin, the colour changes to brown. An encircling band of varying width ornaments the belly.

Rather thin lines fill the uppermost zone. The handle zone is decorated with fine Myc. III flower patterns (FM 18). The top plate shows four concentric circles (including the paint on the rim) with a painted dot and a point (from a compass) in the centre. The strap-handles are painted on the outside, except for a zone left free at the top. A painted band connects neck and spout at the root.

Max. H. : 14.6 cm.

Max. W. : 14.2 cm.

Fig. 46. Stirrup jar 4,10 (Ist. inv.no. 4260) from Passia grave 4. Seen from the side and from above. 1 : 2.

Fig. 47. Piriform ovoid jar 4,11 (Ist. inv.no. 4241) from
Passia grave 4. Photo 1 : 4. Drawing (Helvig Kinch) 1 : 8.

4,11 (Ist. inv.no. 4241) (Fig. 47, Fig. 117). Large piriform ovoid jar with three vertical simple strap-handles (FS 37). Parts of the belly and the rim of the conical neck are missing (restored or intact on Mrs. Kinch's drawing Fig. 47) – the preserved part of the neck is much restored with gypsum. Fabric red. Light yellow slip (peeling), changing in places to a reddish tone. Red/brown paint. The foot and neck are painted, two bands encircle the lower part of the body and three bands are found below the handles. Decoration of running spirals (FM 46) below a fringe of slanting parallel lines. Paint on the outside of the handles – an oval band round the handle.
Max. H. (Kinch) : 45.0 cm.
Max. W. : 33.0 cm.

4,12 (Ist. inv.no. 4268) (Fig. 48, Fig. 120). Shallow, side-spouted (with bridge-spout), semi-globular cup with vertical strap handle and a low ring-foot. Little restoration. The outher surface is covered in a light yellow slip (inside, both paint and slip are rather peeled off). Varying brown/black paint. A band encircles the outside

of the ring-foot. One band on the rim (covering inside and outside) and one below the handle zone. Decorated in the handle zone with parallel slanting lines grouped in ten pairs – one group, however, has three lines. The strap handle and the spout are painted on the outside and on the top, respectively. On the inside, the bowl is decorated with two broad rings painted con-

Fig. 48. Bridge-spouted cup 4,12 (Ist. inv.no. 4268) from Passia grave 4. 1 : 2.

Fig. 49. Coarse-ware jug 4,13 from Passia grave 4. (from Kinch's incomplete manuscript). 2 : 3.

centrically round the centre at the bottom. One is quite close to the bottom, the other approximately at the middle of the belly. Wheel traces at the bottom.
Max. H. : 6.8 cm.
Max. W. (across the handle) : 14.9 cm.

4,13 (not found in Istanbul) (Fig. 49). (Description according to Kinch's unpublished manuscripts). "Small jug with vertical, high-swung handle. Part of rim missing (has there been a spout ?). The fabric is coarse, porous and the colour almost black. No decoration".
Max. H. : 9.0 cm.
Max. W. : 7.4 cm.
Wall : 0.4 cm.

4,14 (Copenh. inv.no. 12366) (Fig. 50). Psi idol. Well preserved. Pink-yellow fabric. Surface covered in creamy yellow, burnished slip. Decorated in brownish-red lustrous paint. The conical top has a band at the rim from which hang continuous semicircles. Around the "head" is an encircling band from which parallel, short hanging lines and parallel, short horizontal lines run down the back of the head. Another band is painted on the nose ridge and round the neck. The eyes are indicated by dots. The breasts are marked. Vertical, curving, parallel bands decorate the arms and the breast zone even on the back. This zone is framed by the neckband and a horizontal band encircling the lower part of the arms. On front and back, a painted line runs down from this band to the bottom of the conical foot.
Max. H. : 11.1 cm.
Max. W. (across the arms) : 15.1 cm.

4,15 (Fig. 51). Various items. According to Kinch's manuscript they were found "at the bottom of the grave close to one of the skulls".

1) "Five blue oblong glass beads" (Copenh., inv.no. 12400). Four, blue, cast glass-paste pendants with spiral decoration and thread-holes bored through top and bottom, surmounted by a line of ribbing [6].

Three coils each with central projection. Two have anti-clockwise coils (c and d), two have clockwise coils (a and b). Slight differences in details of ornamention.

Dimensions:
a) H : 2.9 cm, W : 1.2 cm.
b) H : 3.1 cm, W : 1.1 cm.
c) H : 2.5 cm, W : 1.0 cm.
d) (only the lower part is preserved) H : 1.9 cm, W : 1.0 cm. One fragment of the upper part of a green, cast glass-paste pendant with end pierced by a transverse thread-hole and having a line of ribbing. Rosette pattern in relief – three petals preserved (originally probably five)[7].
Dimensions (preserved):
e) H : 1.1 cm, W : 1.1 cm.

2) Six small reddish-brown and blue glass rings (Copenh. inv.no. 12388) (Fig. 51).
Diameter (outside) : 0.3 cm.
3) Ovoid, glass-paste bead with alternating white and blue encircling stripe. The paste is blue and the white stripes are shallow inlays in the blue paste. (Copenh. inv.no. 12402) (Fig. 51). Part of one side missing.
L. : 1.7 cm, W. : 1.0 cm.
Diam. thread-hole : 0.3 cm.
4) Fragmentarily preserved bead in blue glass-

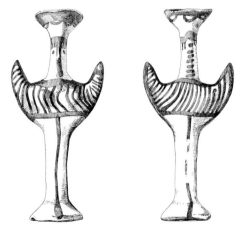

Fig. 50. Psi idol 4,14 (Copenhagen inv.no. 12366) from Passia grave 4. 1 : 2 (from Kinch's incomplete manuscript).

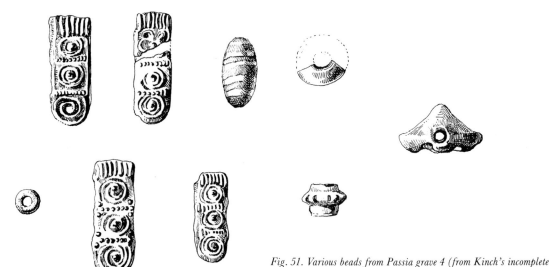

Fig. 51. Various beads from Passia grave 4 (from Kinch's incomplete manuscript). 1 : 1.

paste (as no. 3). (Copenh. inv.no. 12385) (Fig. 51).
H. : 0.9 cm, W. (preserved) : 1.3 cm.
Diam. thread-hole : 0.4 cm.
5) Pointed conical bead in blue glass-paste. Preserved intact. (Copenh. inv.no. 12401) (Fig. 51). The rim curves slightly upwards. Two parallel depressions at the bottom.
H. : 1.3 cm, W. : 2.2 cm.
Diam. hole : 0.3 cm.
6) Small, cylindrical, white glass (?) bead intended to have a relief-band round the middle. (Copenh. inv.no. 12405) (Fig. 51).
H. : 0.4 cm, W. : 0.6 cm.
Diam. of hole : 0.3 cm.
Further "five, small globular faience beads", recorded as Copenh. inv.no. 12404, are said to have been found in Passia Grave H – however, there was no mention of these in K. F. Kinch's manuscript.

Apsaktiras, Vati

From Kinch's files : The cemetery of Apsaktiras was visited by Kinch in May 1904. The site is on the left of the river Vati, some 20 minutes (walk) from the village of Vati. The cemetery had been "excavated" by peasants from Vati for 2–3 weeks in January 1904. It was reported that 25 graves were emptied and c. 280 complete vases were found besides a huge number of broken vases, which were discarded. All graves were Mycenaean (except one – see below), and the dromoi turned E, with a deviation towards SE. (Fig. 52).
Kinch started work in the necropolis on May 17th together with a Turkish delegate. For Epis-

tat he chose a son of the Demarch of Vati, Nicolo Manoli. However, no unopened graves could be found, thus work had to be restricted to cleaning up and measuring some of the graves.
Except for grave 7, which proved to be Hellenistic, all graves were Mycenaean. "In a few instances there had been an entrance from one chamber to another grave". The soil was partly the white "Asproperos", partly clay almost as hard as stone. Thus the graves were well preserved and dry. The dromoi had been carefully dressed with a pointed, rather narrow implement, the scars from which were still visible on the almost vertical walls. The entrance to the dromos was blocked by a stone packing, as was the stomion itself, or by a row of stones only. In one of the best preserved graves, where the finest vases had been found, the floor was paved. Vases had been found in all graves – from 2 to 55 in a grave. The richest graves were in the centre and in the highest positions as found elsewhere (Exochi). Up to seven skeletons had been found in one grave. In one of the graves shown to Kinch four bodies had been found, two at each side of the entrance, with the legs pointing towards the door. Besides vases, the Apsaktiras cemetery only contained bronze weapons and knives, glass ornaments and whetstones. One small bead and two pieces of jewellery in gold foil were found. Little more was found by cleaning the graves : one vase, some glass ornaments and sfondili, as well as bronze knives. Some cleaned and measured graves are described infra.
Note. Not all the information given by Kinch is reliable as he evidently mixed the information given by the peasants with his own genuine field notes.

50

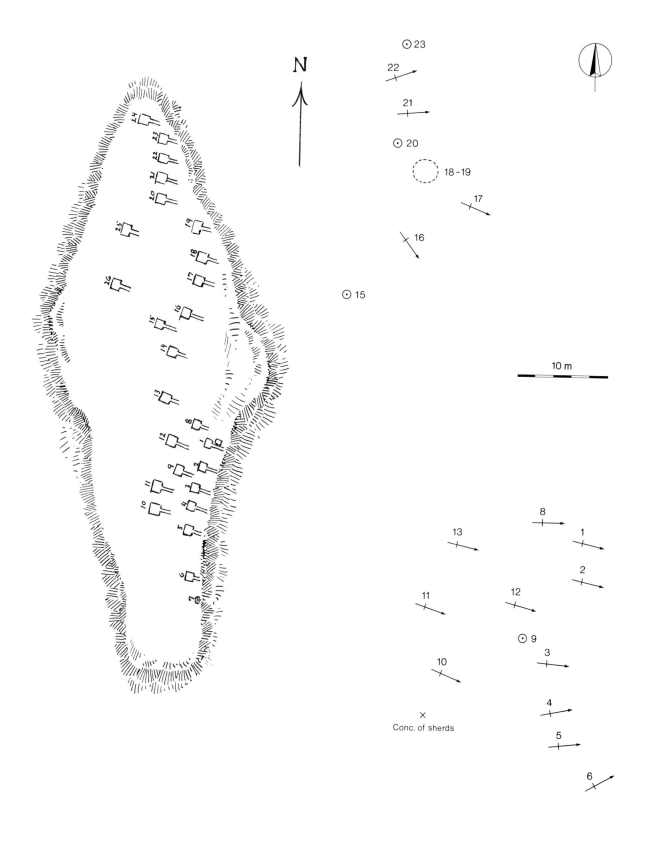

N

⊙ 23
22
21
⊙ 20
⎯⎯⎯⎯ 18-19
17
16
⊙ 15

10 m

8
13   1
              2
11   12
    ⊙ 9
        3
10

×
Conc. of sherds

4
5
6

Fig. 52. The cemetery of Apsaktiras. Sketch from Kinch's incomplete manuscript, and measurements made in 1975.

⊢⎯⎯➤   Direction out of chamber.
        Cross indicating stomion (measuring point).

⊙   Uncertain construction.

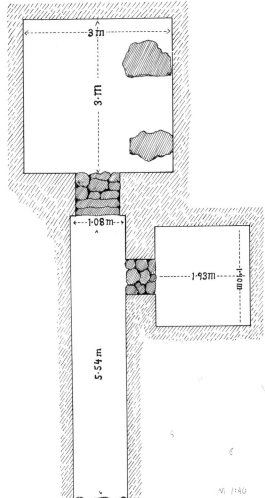

Fig. 53. Apsaktiras grave 1. Drawing and plan from Kinch's incomplete manuscript.

Grave 1 (Fig. 53). L. of dromos : 5.54 m. Orientation, E-W turned slightly S.

W. of dromos at door : 1.08 m.

H. of dromos at door : c. 2.35 m.

H. of stomion : 1.26 m, W. : 0.90 m, L. : 0.85 m. The chamber measured 3 × 3 m. The roof of the chamber was domed. H. above floor : 2.20 m. The vault started 0.92 m above floor level. Two large, flat, oblong stones were found along the northern side of the grave – the upper surface of the stones was corrugated, while the lower was smoothed. Two bodies lay on top of these stones, and a further two bodies were found in the southern part of the grave. According to reports, one of the bodies had had a bronze helmet (sic) at the head. 46 vases should have been found in this grave, mainly in the corners, in a central row and around the skulls. The bronze knife No. 11 (inv.no. 12413) and the three glass ornaments No. 3 (inv.no. 12399) (see infra) were found in this grave.

In the northern wall of the dromos, at a distance of 0.87 m from the door, an entrance was found to a smaller chamber.

W. of door : 0.70, H. : 1.10 m, L. : 0.60 m.

This grave was less important, and only contained 5–6 vases, according to information. As the vault had collapsed, measurements were difficult to estimate.

H. of chamber : 1.80 m.

Grave 2 (Fig. 54). L. of dromos : 5 m.

W. at entrance : 0.72 m.

W. at door : 0.83 m.

H. of dromos at door : 4.68 m.

H. of door : max. 1.12 m.

L. of stomion : 0.75–0.80 m.

The almost square chamber measured : 2 m (E/W), 2.15 m (N/S).

H. of vault : 1.92 m.

"The grave had been opened by the epistat Nicola and contained 18 vases; but this was at

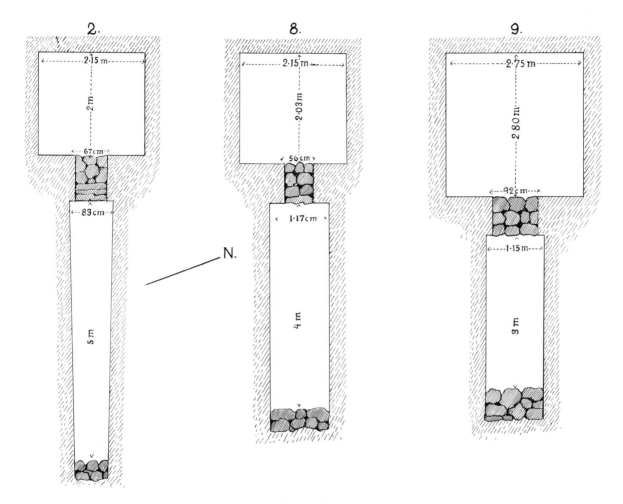

Fig. 54. Apsaktiras graves II, VIII and IX. Plans from Kinch's incomplete manuscript.

nightfall, and the numbers and positions of the bodies were not observed". One skull appeared during the cleaning out of this grave, but it was not found in situ.

Grave 8 (Fig. 54). L. of dromos : c. 4 m.
The chamber had been emptied by the peasants. The roof was vaulted, H. from top of vault to floor : 1.80 m. The walls had been carefully smoothed. Distance to ground surface above vault : c. 0.44 m. The vaulted roof started c. 0.85 m above floor level.

Grave 9 (Fig. 54) The grave had been opened from the roof by the epistat Nicola. The entrance to the dromos was closed by a stone packing, H. : c. 1 m.
L. of dromos : 3 m.
W. : 1.15 m.
H. of dromos at stomion : 2.45 m.
W. of stomion : 0.92 m, H. : 1.19 m., L. : 0.75 m.
Dimensions of chamber : L. 2.85 m × W. : 2.75

m × H. : c. 2 m. As the roof had collapsed, the measurements are not precise.

It was reported that many vases had been found everywhere in the grave. Furthermore, it contained knives, whetstones and 15 green glass beads.

When the cemetery of Apsaktiras was visited in July 1975 (Fig. 55) it was rather characteristic that the elevation was separated into an upper (northern) and a lower (southern) plateau, the boundary running between graves 14 and 15. Most graves were rather poorly preserved, as the roofs had collapsed in almost all cases. Grave 11 was rather special as it had niches cut in the side walls of the dromos close to the stomion.

Some finds from the necropolis of Apsaktiras were purchased from the peasants (grave 21), some found by Kinch when cleaning out the graves. As far as possible the provenance is given separately for each piece.

Fig. 55. The cemetery of Apsaktiras from the North. Chamber tomb no. 22 in the foreground (July 17th, 1975).

Catalogue of grave goods

(the numbers follow those in Kinch's catalogue).

Pottery

1 (Copenh. inv.no. 12365) (Fig. 56, Fig. 121). Deep bowl with low foot (FS 284). One handle is badly damaged and a sherd is missing at the rim. Pink fine fabric. The surface is covered in a light reddish-yellow, burnished slip. Wheel traces are clearly seen on the surface. Reddish-brown lustrous paint. A band round the foot.

Two horizontal parallel bands below the handles limit the handle zone downwards. Between the handles the decoration consists of antithetic spiral patterns (FM 50) executed rather carelessly. The pattern filling in the triglyphs is made up of horizontal wavy lines. The handles are decorated with drop patterns and the rim has a band. Inside the bowl there are five concentric circles painted around the centre at the bottom, and a band is painted on the rim.

Max. H. : 7.0 cm.

Max. W. : 10.4 cm.

Max. W. (across handles : 16.0 cm).

Prov. : grave 11.

54

Fig. 56. Deep bowl no. 1 (Copenhagen inv.no. 12365) from Apsaktiras grave 11. 1 : 2.

2 (Copenh. inv.no. 7554) (Fig. 57). Askoid jar with flat-sectioned loop handle and hole at one end (FS 194). Preserved complete. Yellow burnished slip. Dark brown paint. The body is decorated with an irregular frame, following the outline of the jar; within the frame is a pattern of parallel, slightly waving lines. On the bottom are three zones with parallel wavy lines, parallel lines and crosses framed by parallel lines; near the front spout parallel lines run transversely for the length of the jar. A similar pattern is at the top of the jar and on top of the handle.
Max. H. : 6.5 cm.
Max. W. : 9.4 cm.
Published : *CVA*, DK, Pl. 46.10.
Prov. : "– from grave 21".

3 (Copenh. inv.no. 7561) (Fig. 58, Fig. 118). Globular bottle with a low foot, where a standing-ring is indicated by a very shallow concavity (FS 198). Two flat-sectioned vertical handles run

from body to spout. Part of one handle is restored and part of the lip is missing. The paint is rather poorly preserved. Light yellow fabric. A light yellow, rather rich slip is poorly preserved. Decorated in reddish-brown paint. Several broader horizontal bands framing thinner parallel lines originally encircled the body – but are poorly preserved. A band on the small ring-foot. Six tongue patterns of semicircular execution (FM 19.29) in the handle zone. Ring around the base of the neck. The outside of the handles was originally painted in monochrome, but only traces of this remain.
Max. H. : 10.6 cm.
Max. W. : 8.2 cm.
Published : *CVA*, DK, Pl. 48.6.
Prov. : "– from grave 21".

4 (Copenh. inv.no. 7559) (Fig. 59, Fig. 116). Small, globular, perked-up stirrup jar with small ring-foot (the ring-base is clearly marked – but the concavity is rather shallow, (FS 176). Handles of oval section. Spout missing. Light yellow-pink fabric. The surface is covered in a thin, light, reddish-brown slip, slightly burnished. Varying reddish-brown, matt paint. Three bands encircle the belly. The decoration in the

Fig. 57. Askos no. 2 (Copenhagen inv.no. 7554) from Apsaktiras "grave 21". 1 : 2.

Fig. 58. Globular bottle no. 3 (Copenhagen inv.no. 7561) from Apsaktiras "grave 21". 1 : 2.

Fig. 59. Globular stirrup jar no. 4 (Copenhagen inv.no. 7559) from Apsaktiras "grave 21". Seen from the side and from above. 1 : 2.

and spout are connected by an oval band. Five horizontal strokes of paint decorate the top of each handle. At the top of the false neck, which is slightly depressed, is a spiral around a central boss.

Max. H. : 11.2 cm.
Max. W. : 10.2 cm.
Published : *CVA*, DK, P. 60.12.
Prov. : "– from grave 21".

5 (Copenh. inv.no. 12367) (Fig. 60). Psi idol. A few sherds are missing from the conical top, otherwise it is complete. Decoration on the back is virtually nonexistent, but paint on the front is well preserved. The fabric is greyish with a faint

handle zone consists of three parallel chevron patterns (FM 58) in an unusual curved execution (five in each group). In the area opposite the spout, this pattern is surrounded by dots. Neck

Fig. 60. Psi idol no. 5 (Copenhagen inv.no. 12367) from Apsaktiras "grave 21". (drawing by Helvig Kinch). 1 : 2.

Fig. 61. Kylikes and small bowl from Apsaktiras "grave 21" (from Kinch's incomplete manuscript). 7, 1 : 2, 8, 1 : 5, 6, 1 : 3.

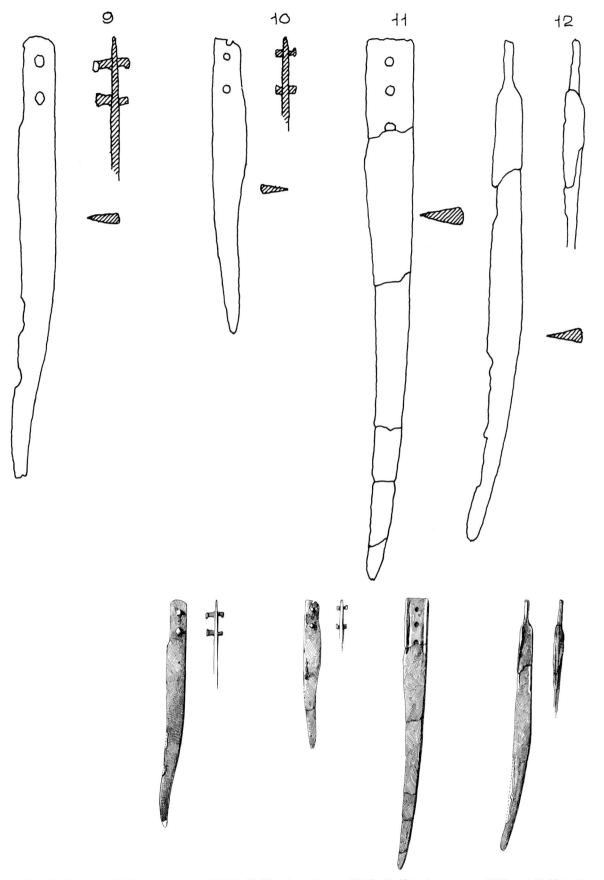

Fig. 62. Knives nos. 9 (Copenhagen inv.no. 12414), 10 (Copenhagen inv.no. 12416), 11 (Copenhagen inv.no. 12413) and 12 (Copenhagen inv.no. 12417). All from Apsaktiras. (Tracing and drawing by Helvig Kinch). 1 : 2 and 1 : 4.

yellow tinge. The surface is covered in a rich, light yellow, burnished slip. Rich black (or very dark brown) changing to reddish-brown lustrous paint. The decoration is identical to that of the idol from Passia grave 4, 14 (supra p. 49).
Max. H. : 11.7 cm.
Max. W. (across the arms) : 5.1 cm.
Prov. : "– from grave 21".

6 (not identified in Istanbul or in Copenhagen) (Fig. 61). Kinch gives the following description : "Undecorated kylix, H. : 0.18 m, with two vertical handles and fragments of two similar. Clay dark yellowish, burnished".
Prov. : "– from grave 21".

7 (not identified in Istanbul or in Copenhagen) (Fig. 61). Kinch gives the following description : "Smaller undecorated kylix with two handles, H. : 0.095 m".
Prov. : "– from grave 21".

8 (not identified in Istanbul or in Copenhagen) (Fig. 61). Kinch gives the following description : "Undecorated bowl, H. 0.07 m, Diam. : 0.17 m".
Prov. : "– from grave 21".

Bronzes

9 (Copenh. inv.no. 12414) (Fig. 62). Bronze knife with one cutting-edge. Part of the edge and the point missing. The flat haft zone is very clearly indicated, with a convex termination, and fragments of the originally organic haft are still preserved. Two nails are still in situ. The haft zone is only 4.7 cm in length. The curving blade has a thick back and evidently the point turned upwards.
L. (as preserved) : 22.5 cm.
Max. W. : 1.8 cm.
L. nails : 1.5 cm.
D. nails : 0.4 cm.

10 (Copenh. inv.no. 12416) (Fig. 62). Bronze knife with one cutting-edge. The top of the handle is broken off. The haft zone, L. : 4.0 cm, is clearly marked; it is flat with sporadically slightly raised edges. Two nails preserved. The slightly thick back of the blade curves somewhat – the edge has evidently been sharpened.
L. : 15.1 cm.
Max. W. : 1.9 cm.
L. nails : 1.1 – 1.2 cm.
D. nails : 0.2 cm.

11 (Copenh. inv.no. 12413) (Fig. 62). Bronze knife with one cutting edge. Only a few frag-

ments are missing. Straight termination to handle. The handle zone, L. : 6.4 cm, with three nail holes, has raised edges. The thick back of the blade curves slightly.
L. : 28.0 cm.
Max. W. : 2.5 cm.
W. of back (blade) : 1.0 cm.
Max. W. of raised edges on haft : 0.9 cm.
D. of nail holes : 0.3 cm.
Prov. : "Apsaktiras gr. 1".

12 (Copenh. inv.no. 12417) (Fig. 62). Bronze knife with one cutting-edge. Fragments missing from the blade and haft. The handle zone, L. 10.0 cm (point included), terminates in a long point. The haft is framed by raised edges produced by the same technique as used for the sword Passia grave 2 (supra p. 34). Fragments of an organic inlay can be seen, no nail holes. The curving blade has a thick back and the edge has probably been sharpened.
L. (preserved) : 26.4 cm.
Max. W. : 1.8 cm.
W. of back (blade) : 0.5 cm.
Max W. of raised edges on haft : 1.1 cm.
Prov. : Gr 1. (?).

Glass ornaments

1 (Copenh. inv.no. 12398) (Fig. 63, Fig. 64). Seven, blue, cast glass-paste pendants ("Curls of hair") with spiral decoration and two thread-holes bored through top and bottom. One is slightly damaged. All spirals coil clockwise and are surmounted by a line of ribbing. The pendants are almost identical.
L. : 3.0 cm.
W. : 0.9 cm.

2 (Copenh. inv.no. 12397) (Fig. 63, Fig. 64). Four blue and three green, cast glass-paste pendants ("Curls of hair") in shape of single curls depending from a rectangular headpiece. Thread-holes through top and bottom. Two rows of bobbles at the top plate, and bobbles framing the curl[8].
The pendants are almost identical.
Prov. : "Found in grave 9 in SW corner round a skull".

3 (Copenh. inv.no. 12399) (Fig. 63). Three rosette-discs in blue glass-paste with two transverse thread-holes. Eight petals in the rosette.
Two are larger : D. : 2.5 cm.
One is smaller : D. : 2.1 cm.
Prov. : The two larger : "grave 1 ?"

4 (no. not used).

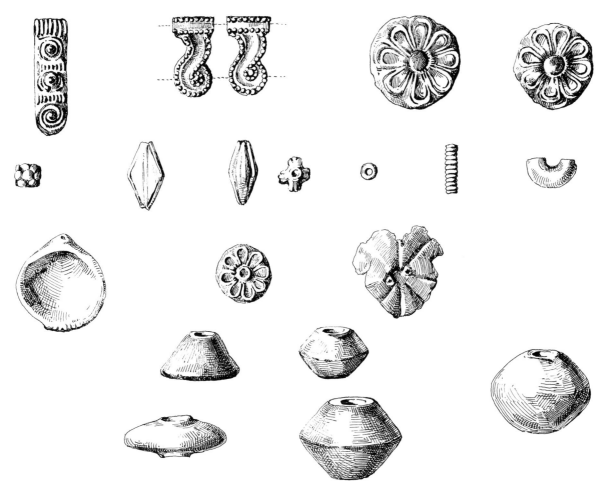

Fig. 63. Glass ornaments, gold beads/ornaments, stone and clay beads from Apsaktiras (drawing by Helvig Kinch, from the incomplete manuscript). 1 : 1.

5 (Copenh. inv.no. 12395) (Fig. 63). Two green and one blue rhomboid (seed-shaped, "grain of wheat") cast faience beads, "spacers", for a necklace. Thread-hole through the longitudinal axis. Decorated with straight lines.
L. : 1.7 – 1.9 cm.
W. : 1.0 cm.
Prov. : "Found in two graves – two from grave 9".

6 (Copenh. inv.no. 12403) (Fig. 63). One green/ light blue cast faience bead with star-shaped section. Thread-hole through the longitudinal axis.
L. : 1.5 cm.
Max. W. : 0.9 cm.

7 (Copenh. inv.no. 12389) (Fig. 63). 29 small faience beads – red, blue and a few yellow.
D. : 0.2 cm.
Prov. : "Found in the same place". Only 19 beads, however, are mentioned in Kinch's sketchbook.

8 (Copenh. inv.no. 12387) (Fig. 63). Eight more or less fragmentarily preserved oblong faience beads[9].
Thread-hole in the longitudinal axis.
Max. L. : 1.2 cm.
Max. W. : 0.3 cm.

9 Bead of glass ? (not identified).

Gold beads and ornaments

1 (Copenh. inv.no. 12396) (Fig. 63). Small, cylindrical, granulated (?) gold bead with thread-hole.
H. : 0.3 cm.

2 (Copenh. inv.no. 12394) (Fig. 63). Copper or bronze (not gold) foil with rosette pattern. Eight petals round a circular centre in relief. Traces of casting at the centre of the reverse.
D. : 1.5 cm.

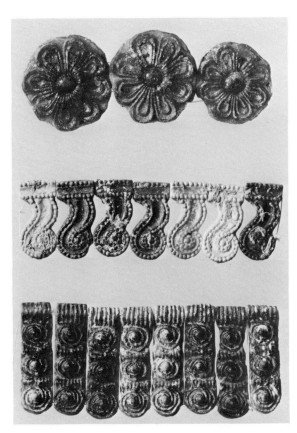

Fig. 64. Glass ornaments 1 (Copenhagen inv.no. 12398), 2 (Copenhagen inv.no. 12397) and 5 (Copenhagen inv.no. 12395). 1 : 1.

3 (Copenh. inv.no. 12394) (Fig. 63). Piece of thin gold foil, fragmentarily preserved. Pattern of eight grooved lines radiating from a circular grooved centre. Two perforations for fixing at the edge of the central groove.
Max. D : 2.5 cm.

Stone and clay beads

1 (Copenh. inv.no. 12390–91) (Fig. 63). One almost totally intact and one partly intact conical bead made of black, homogeneous stone (basalt ?).
D. : 2.1 cm.
H. (of intact bead) : 1.1 cm.
H. (of fragmentary bead) : 1.0 cm.
Thread-hole D. : 0.4 cm.

2 (Copenh. inv.no. 12383) (Fig. 63). Double-cone, truncated bead made of black, homogeneous stone (like no. 1). The thread-hole is positioned rather off centre at one end.
H. : 1.3 cm.
D. : 1.9 cm.
Thread-hole D. : 0.5 cm.

3 (Copenh. inv.no. 12392) (Fig. 63). Double-cone, truncated bead (?) or spindle whorl made of brownish stone (?). The thread-hole is positioned rather off centre at one end.
H. : 2.1 cm.
D. : 2.7 cm.

4 (Copenh. inv.no. 12393) (Fig. 63). Flat, circular bead of clay. Light pink fabric. Upper surface convex.
H. : 1.0 cm.
D. : 2.7 cm.
Thread-hole D. : 0.4 cm.

5 (Copenh. inv.no. 12384) (Fig. 63). Double-cone, truncated bead.
H. : 2.1 cm.
D. : 2.8 cm.
Thread-hole D. : 0.5 cm.

Catalogue of survey material

Grave 2

(Fig. 65). Rim fragment of an open bowl – probably a kylix. Brown fabric. Surface covered in yellow slip. Paint on rim and horizontal lines on body in brown/dark red.
Estimated diam. : 14 cm.
Dimensions : 4.0 × 5.0 cm.

Near Grave 11

No. 1 (Fig. 66). Side sherd from an open-shaped jar, the inside surface is corrugated. Brownish-red (5 YR 7/8) fabric. The surface inside and out is covered in a thick, rich, dark yellow (7.5 YR 7/6), burnished slip. Decorated in black lustrous paint – a rhomboid chequer pattern grid, every other row being filled wih parallel chevrons.
Dimensions : 8.3 × 5.1 cm.

No. 2 Same category of ware as No. 1. Probably a piece from neck of jar or jug. Horizontal bands in black paint.
Dimensions : 5.0 × 2.7 cm.

No. 3 (Fig. 66). Side fragment from upper part of an open-shaped, slightly incurved krater (?). Dark red fabric. The inside surface is neatly smoothed, that on the outside covered in a light yellow slip. Decoration in black (badly peeled) paint consisting of panelled pattern of wavy lines issuing from a broad band. Another panel starts to the left.
Dimensions : 6.2 × 4.5 cm.

No. 4. (Fig. 66). Fragment of upper part of stirrup jar – traces of handle or spout projection on

60

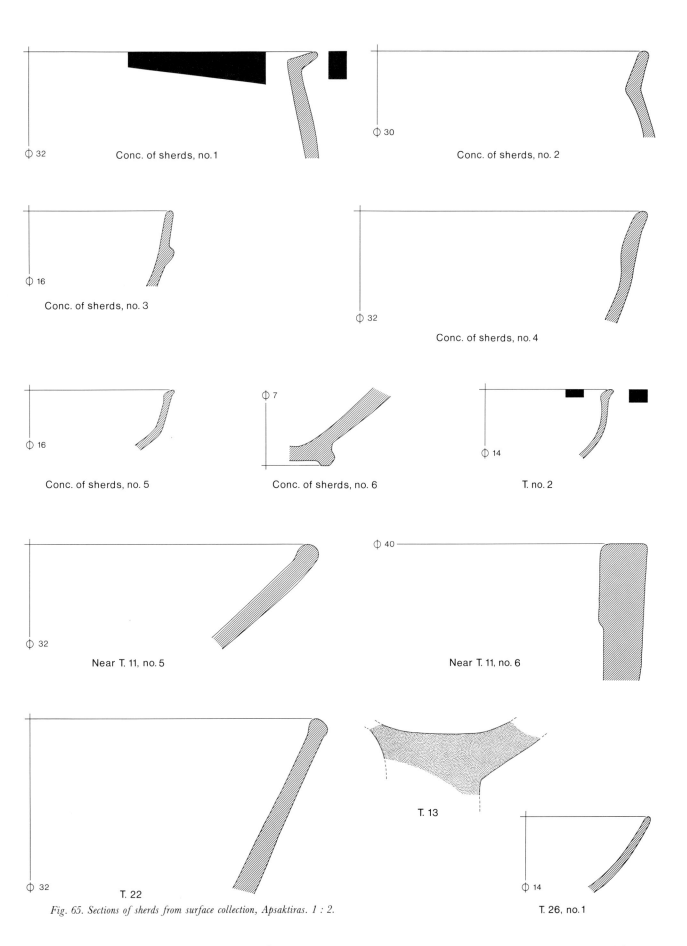

Ø 32 Conc. of sherds, no. 1

Ø 30 Conc. of sherds, no. 2

Ø 16 Conc. of sherds, no. 3

Ø 32 Conc. of sherds, no. 4

Ø 16 Conc. of sherds, no. 5

Ø 7 Conc. of sherds, no. 6

Ø 14 T. no. 2

Ø 32 Near T. 11, no. 5

Ø 40 Near T. 11, no. 6

Ø 32 T. 22

T. 13

Ø 14 T. 26, no. 1

Fig. 65. Sections of sherds from surface collection, Apsaktiras. 1 : 2.

61

Fig. 66. Sherds found "Near Grave 11" at Apsaktiras. (The two to the left are Turkish). 1 : 2.

the upper band. Sandwiched fabric. The outer surface covered in a rich, light yellow slip; brownish-red paint. Bands and thinner lines. Handle zone decorated with parallel chevrons — diameter of handle zone c. 8 cm.
Dimensions : 4.5 × 4.5 cm.
Various side fragments of open and closed shapes with horizontal bands and lines (6 pieces, only 5 depicted) (Fig. 67).

No. 5 (Fig. 65, Fig. 66). Rim fragment of an open

Fig. 68. Sherds from jug. Apsaktiras grave 13. 1 : 2.

bowl in coarse ware. Grey, very fine and dense fabric. The red surface is smoothed showing lines of incised vertical strokes made with some sort of implement (Turkish).
Estimated diam. : 24 cm.
Dimensions : 7.2 × 6.5 cm.

No. 6 (Fig. 65). Rim fragment of large pithos with thickened rim. Coarse red fabric.
Estimated diam. : 40 cm.
Dimensions : 7.3 × 10.5 cm.
– Three coarse ware sherds, one of which has incisions like those on No. 5 (Fig. 66).

Grave 13

(Fig. 65, Fig. 68). Side fragment and fragment of spout of jug. Fragment of handle attachment from the side opposite to the spout – attached to rim. Buff fabric (7.5 YR 7/6). Outside surface covered in light yellow (10 YR 7/4) slip, slightly burnished. Encircling bands and lines round the

Fig. 67. Various sherds from "Near Grave 11" at Apsaktiras. 1 : 2.

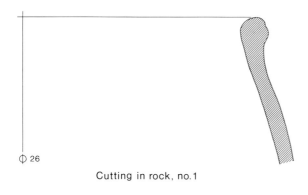

○ 26

Cutting in rock, no.1

○ 22

Various finding places, no.1

Fig. 69. Sections of sherds from surface collection. Apsaktiras. 1 : 2.

belly in reddish-brown (5 YR 5/69) paint. Painted band below the rim varies between 1½ and 2 cm in width. Top of rim painted.

Grave 22

(Fig. 65). Rim fragment of large open jar (bowl ?) with thickened rim. The fabric has a grey core framed by dark brown. Brown, smooth surface with two parallel, horizontally incised, encircling lines.
Estimated diam. : 32 cm.
Dimensions : 10.2 × 11.7 cm.

Grave 26

No. 1 (Fig. 65). Small bowl. Reddish-yellow (7.5 YR 7/6) fabric. Reddish-yellow, smoothed surface.
Estimated diam. : 14 cm.
Dimensions : 5.1 × 4.4 cm.

Cutting in rock south of East 90.5, North 118 (SE of Concentration of Sherds).

No. 1 (Fig. 69, Fig. 70). Rim sherd of large krater. Reddish-yellow (5 YR 6/6) fabric. Outside covered in black (2.5 YR 5/8) lustrous paint – traces of red paint inside.

No. 2 (Fig. 70). Side fragment of a large closed-shape jar. Reddish-yellow (7.5 YR 6/8) fabric. Yellow (10 YR 8/6), slightly burnished slip on

outside. Red (2.5 YR 5/8) lustrous paint – spiral pattern and scale pattern (FM 70).
Dimensions : 9.9 × 7.2 cm.

No. 3 (Fig. 70). Side fragment of open-shaped (?) jar. Pale yellow (2.5 Y 8/4) fabric. Surface covered in pale yellow slip with black painted diaper net (FM 57) issuing from a band.
Dimensions : 5.0 × 3.1 cm.
– Three sherds with encircling band and line decoration (one depicted on Fig. 70).

Various finding places

No. 1 (Fig. 69, Fig. 71). Flat dish. Brown coarse fabric.
Smoothed surface.
Estimated diam. : 22 cm.
Dimensions : 7.5 × 5.7 cm.

No. 2 (Fig. 71). Side fragment of closed-shape jar. Very pale brown (10 YR 7/4) fabric. Surface covered in a very pale brown (10 YR 8/4 – somewhat more yellow) burnished slip. Red paint – diaper grid – tassel, a dot and encircling band.
Dimensions : 7.1 × 4.8 cm.

No. 3 (Fig. 71) Side fragment of closed-shape jar. Light red (2.5 YR 6/6) fabric. The surface covered in a very pale brown or yellow slip. Reddish-brown (5 YR 5/4) lustrous paint. Zone of parallel chevrons (FM 58), broad bands and

Fig. 70. Sherds from surface collection : "Cutting in Rock", Apsaktiras. 1 : 2.

Fig. 71. Sherds from surface collection : "Various finding-places". Apsaktiras. 1 : 2.

panelled patterns with wavy line motif and a stemmed spiral (FM 51).
Dimension : 8.5 × 8.5 cm.

Concentration of sherds in Mycenaean Necropolis

No. 1 (Fig. 65, Fig. 72). Rim fragment of large krater. Red coarse fabric. Inner and outer surface covered in reddish-yellow (7.5 YR 7/6), burnished slip. Decorated with dark reddish-brown (5 YR 3/3) paint on rim, outside and in, and isolated semicircles (FM 43).

Fig. 72. Sherds from surface collection : "Concentration of sherds in Mycenaean Necropolis", Apsaktiras. (Upper row, left : 1, right : 3, lower row, left : 4, right : 2). 1 : 2.

Estimated diam. : 32 cm.
Dimensions : 5.8 × 10.0 cm.

No. 2 (Fig. 65, Fig. 72). Rim fragment of krater with traces of handle at rim. Brownish-red fabric. The inside is covered in a rich reddish-yellow (7.5 YR 7/6), burnished slip. The slip on the outside is somewhat paler (perhaps the result of a later refiring). Reddish-brown (2.5 YR 4/4), lustrous paint. Motif?
Estimated diam. : 30 cm.
Dimensions : 4.4 × 5.0 cm.

No. 3 (Fig. 65, Fig. 72). Rim fragment of open cup or bowl, with traces of handle. Pink (7.5 YR 7/4) fabric. Smoothed, slightly burnished surface.
Estimated diam. : 16 cm.
Dimensions : 4.4 × 5.7 cm.

No. 4 (Fig. 65, Fig. 72). Rim fragment of coarse ware, open-shaped jar. Very dense red (2.5 YR 5/6) fabric, coarse-tempered. Smoothed surface.
Estimated diam. : 32 cm.
Dimensions : 6.0 × 10.0 cm.

No. 5 (Fig. 65). Rim fragment of kylix bowl. Pink (7.5 YR 7/4) fabric. Smoothed surface.
Estimated diam. : 16 cm.
Dimensions : 3.9 × 4.1 cm.

No. 6 (Fig. 65). Bottom fragment with ring-foot – closed shape (?). Grey fabric. Rings encircling lower part of belly. Colours cannot be established because of refiring.
Dimensions : see section diam.

No. 7 (Fig. 73). Three side fragments from closed-shape jar with decoration in triangles – all from same jar. Sandwich fabric – pink (7.5 YR 7/4) inside, yellow (10 YR 7/6) outside. Very pale brown (10 YR 7/4) slip, slightly burnished. Red (2.5 YR 5/6) paint. One sherd shows transition to neck.

No. 7a (Fig. 73). Sherd with fragment of strap handle, probably from same jar as No. 7.

No. 8 (Fig. 74). Side fragment from closed-shape jar. Pink fabric (7.5 YR 7/4). Light red (2.5 YR 6/6), lustrous paint. Encircling lines and debased wavy line pattern.
Dimensions : 6.0 × 6.0 cm.

No. 8a (Fig. 74). Probably from same jar as No. 8. Drops or debased tassel motif.
Dimensions : 3.7 × 5.0 cm.

No. 9 (Fig. 74). Side fragment of closed-shape jar. Very pale brown (10 YR 7/3) fabric. Yellow (10 YR 7/6), burnished slip on outside. Light red

Fig. 73. Sherds from surface collection : "Concentration of sherds in Mycenaean Necropolis", Apsaktiras. (Upper row, left 7a, right 7, lower row : 7). 1 : 2.

Fig. 75. Sherds from surface collection : "Concentration of sherds in Mycenaean Necropolis", Apsaktiras. (Lower row right, no. 11). 1 : 2.

(2.5 YR 6/6), lustrous paint. Panelled pattern with parallel lines and vertical wavy lines.
Dimensions : 4.1 × 6.2 cm.

No. 10 (Fig. 74). Side fragment of closed-shape jar. Very pale brown (10 YR 7/4) fabric. Reddish-yellow (7.5 YR 7/6), lustrous slip. Red (2.5 YR 5/8), lustrous paint – spiral pattern and band.
Dimensions : 5.1 × 7.8 cm.

No. 10a (Fig. 74). Side fragment of closed-shape jar. Yellow fabric. Yellow (10 YR 7/6), bur-

Fig. 74. Sherds from surface collection : "Concentration of sherds in Mycenaean Necropolis", Apsaktiras. (Upper row, left : 8, right : 8a, mid : 9). 1 : 2.

nished slip. Red (2.5 YR 5/8) paint in a spiral pattern.
Dimensions : 2.8 × 2.9 cm.

No. 11 (Fig. 75). Side fragment with bulb (carination) – closed-shape jar. Very pale brown (10 YR 7/4) fabric. Very pale brown (10 YR 8/4), burnished slip. Reddish-brown (5 YR 5/4), lustrous paint on carination, and dot or tassel.
Estimated diam. round carination : 30 cm.
Dimensions : 3.1 × 4.4 cm.

– A further six sherds are shown on the photographs (Figs. 74–75) – among them one from the discoid foot of a painted kylix. (Fig. 75, upper right corner). The general impression given by the material other than that mentioned (a further 60 sherds were collected) is :
– a large amount is decorated with encircling bands and lines.
– fragments of strap handles and rounded handles (for smaller vases).
– part of a discoid plate and stem from an unpainted kylix.

Kalovriou, Vati

On May 19th, 1904, Kinch and six workmen surveyed a small elevation called Kalovriou, on the left side of the Vati valley – 15 minutes' walk from Vati – approximately opposite the monastery of Galatusa (Fig. 1).
Here graves had been found and emptied by the peasants. The graves were in a bad state of preservation.

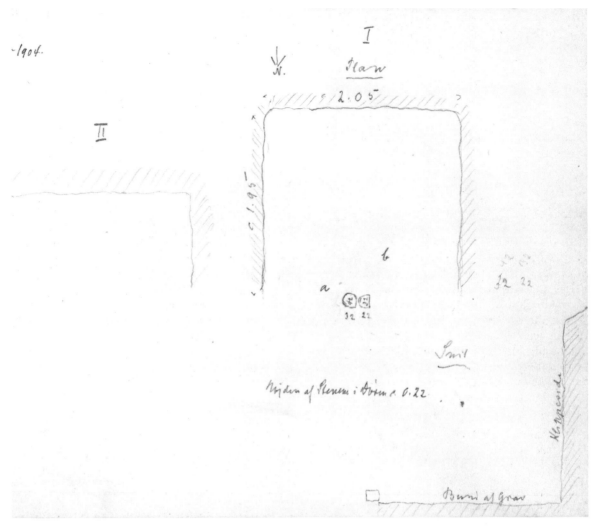

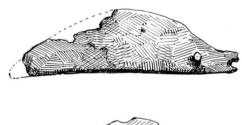

Fig. 76. From Kinch's sketchbook, sketches of Sto Kalovriou graves I-II. Razor and whetstone from grave I (from the incomplete manuscript) – the reconstruction of the razor is probably incorrect. Both items 1 : 2.

However, Mycenaean sherds were collected from the area. The dromos turned to the south. It was reported that the razor and whetstone (Fig. 76) had been found below a skull in grave I. Further finds had been a small vase (a on plan Fig. 76) and the large kylix with the birds ("which I have bought") (b on plan Fig. 76) – this must be the kylix *CVA* DK 2, Pl. 53,8, which was previously in Kinch's private collection, purchased in 1904 with provenance Vati. It was claimed that the outer wall had been built of stones – but Kinch was evidently sceptical.

Bones and Mycenaean sherds were found in the poorly preserved grave II.

During the 1975 survey this site could not be identified.

A2 The Apollakia area

Extracted from Kinch's unpublished manuscript: In February 1904 Kinch visited Apollakia in order to get an impression of various cemeteries in the surroundings, primarily all those from the late Mycenaean Period that had been found and excavated by the peasants. Numerous graves were found in the area, usually situated on small elevations. Especially between Apollakia and Monolithos, at Trapezi, there were cemeteries containing attractive, well-preserved vases, but quite a few of them were found to be empty too. Usually, the graves lay scattered around, and only one larger necropolis was found, to the north of Apollakia on a hill called Stous Milous. This cemetery was visited by Kinch, but evidently all the graves were empty. All were Mycenaean, cut in the soft rock, and typical examples of chambers with dromoi were seen. Often the roofs of the graves had fallen in and here the broken vases were found. The sherds from the site were all Mycenaean "and from the same period", no terracotta idols or bronzes were found. The grave entrances faced East. Dromoi up to 15 metres long were found and they sloped downwards towards the door. "The floor in the graves was situated around ½ meter below the door". Between 1000 and 2000 graves were reported to have been opened in this district.

During the 1975 survey a slight hill with a flat sloping top (a τραπέζι) to the West (NW) of Apollakia, south of the river, was shown to us by a farmer from Apollakia. The name Stous Milous was not recognized by the inhabitants of the village but old people could recall that quite a number of mills had previously existed along the riverside. As the site mentioned was the largest Mycenaean necropolis in the area, we identified the site now called Trapezies Paraelis with that (Stous Milous) recorded by Kinch (Fig. 77). The soil was soft and the graves could

usually only be identified as depressions in the ground – furthermore, the trapezi was rather overgrown by scrub. On the sketch (Fig. 78) only graves definitely identified as such are marked. All identified dromoi turn SE. Where the dromoi could be studied, the side walls sloped outwards towards the bottom. A certain number of sherds were collected from the various graves (chamber or dromos) at the site called Trapezies Paraelis.

Catalogue of survey material
Grave 1

No. 1 (Fig. 79, Fig. 80). Rim and bottom sherd from open bowl with flat bottom or a rather small, low foot. Splayed rim. The fabric (reddish-yellow (7.5 YR 8/6)) is fine-tempered and brownish-pink. The surface is covered in a white (10 YR 8/2), rich (creamy), slightly burnished slip. Decoration in brownish-orange (10 R 6/8 (light red)), lustrous paint. The outside of the rim is covered by a 1.5 cm broad band, the inside by a 1.1 cm broad band. The paint on the top of the rim has peeled off. There are fragments of a running spiral motif (FM 46), probably a lily (FM 9) on the outside. The outside of the bottom sherd shows concentric circles, the inside a flower pattern (FM 18) (Fig. 79). Fragmentarily preserved traces of brown paint are found on the flower. The bottom must have been rather flat as the sherd curves only slightly. (Shape ?).
Estimated diam. : 18 cm.
Max. diam. rim sherd : 6.4 × 3.2 cm.
Max. diam. bottom : 4.0 × 3.2 cm.

No. 2 (Fig. 79, Fig. 80). Rim sherd of kylix (?) with deep bowl. The rim is slightly thickened, and flared. Reddish-brown (7.5 YR 7/6), fine-tempered fabric. The surface is covered in a

Fig. 77. The necropolis of Trapezies Paraelis from the North (July 1975).

reddish-brown (5 R 6/6) slip, slightly burnished on the outside, while the inside is rather matt. Reddish-brown (10 R 5/8 (red)), lustrous paint. The rim is covered by a band – 0.6 cm deep on the outside, 0.7 cm on the inside. Decorated on the outside with multiple stem (FM 19, 26–29) and another motif difficult to interpret as much fragmented.
Estimated diam. : 14 cm.
Max. dimensions : 2.6 (4) × 3.2 cm.

No. 3 (Fig. 79, Fig. 80). Bottom sherd with ring-foot and side sherd from a closed-shape jar. Fine-tempered, reddish-brown fabric. The surface is covered with a light brown burnished slip. Decorated with encircling, alternating broad bands and thinner lines in brown, lustrous paint.
Estimated diam. of ring-foot (outside). 10 cm.
Max. dimensions of ring-foot : 9.5 × 7.0 cm.

No. 4 (Fig. 80). Side sherd of closed-shape jar. The fabric is "sandwiched", the outside half of the wall being red, the inside light brown. The surface is covered in a pink, lustrous slip. Bands of a reddish-brown, lustrous paint.
Max. dimensions : 4.5 × 4.2 cm.

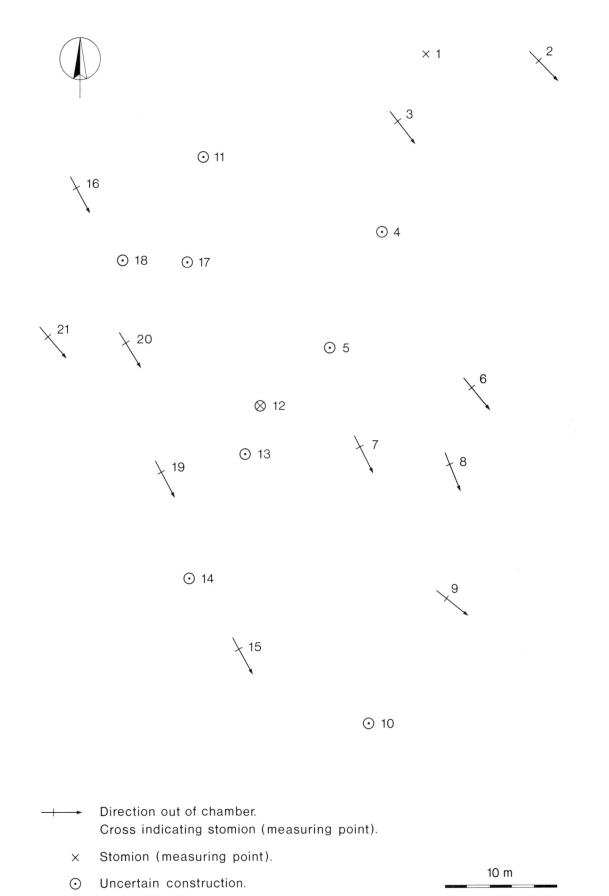

× 1

2

3

⊙ 11

16

⊙ 4

⊙ 18   ⊙ 17

21   20   ⊙ 5

6

⊗ 12

⊙ 13   7

19   8

⊙ 14

9

15

⊙ 10

⊢────▶ Direction out of chamber.
        Cross indicating stomion (measuring point).

×   Stomion (measuring point).

⊙   Uncertain construction.

10 m

Fig. 78 Sketch of the Mycenaean necropolis of Trapezies Paraelis at Apollakia (July 1975).

69

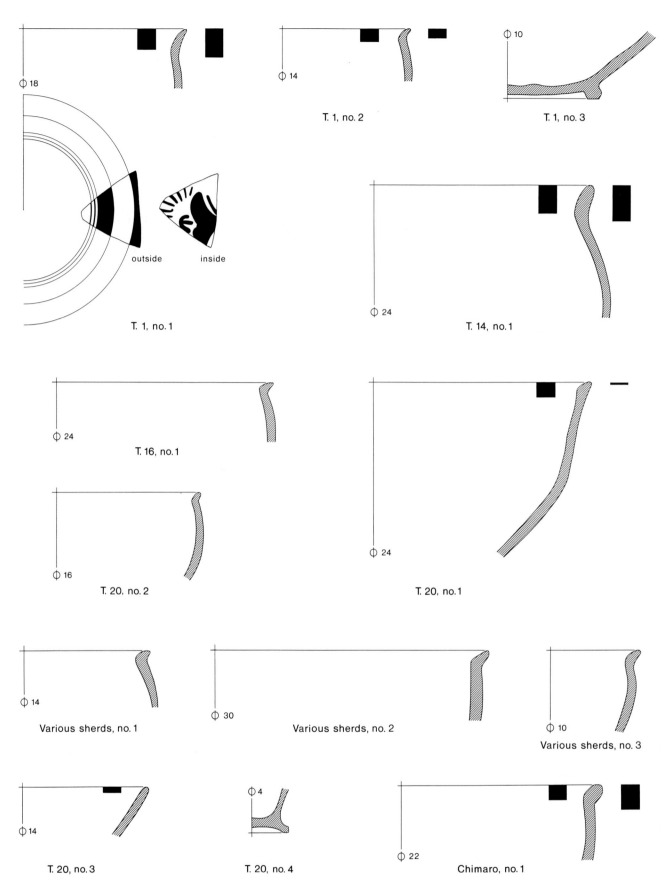

T. 1, no. 2

T. 1, no. 3

outside   inside

T. 1, no. 1

T. 14, no. 1

T. 16, no. 1

T. 20, no. 2

T. 20, no. 1

Various sherds, no. 1

Various sherds, no. 2

Various sherds, no. 3

T. 20, no. 3

T. 20, no. 4

Chimaro, no. 1

Fig. 79. Drawings of sherds from surface collection made at Trapezies Paraelis and Chimaro, Apollakia. 1 : 2.

Fig. 80. Sherds from Trapezies Paraelis grave 1 (2 sherds in upper right corner no. 1, left corner : 2, upper left : no. 3, lower right : no. 4). 1 : 2.

Fig. 82. Sherds from Trapezies Paraelis grave 11. (Upper row left : no. 4, right : no. 5, mid row, left : no. 1, mid : no. 6, – lower row, 2 from left : no. 3, 3 from left : no. 2). 1 : 2. (mid row left should perhaps be seen upside-down).

Grave 3

No. 1 (Fig. 81). Side sherd from a closed-shape, large, rather straight-sided jar. Tile-red (10 R 6/8 (light red)) fabric. The surface is covered in a cream coloured, almost marbled, matt slip (7.5 YR 8/2). Broad bands of black, altering to dark brown paint.
Max. dimensions : 14.1 (H) × 9.5 cm.

Grave 6

No. 1 (Fig. 81). Carinated belly fragment of

Fig. 81. Various sherds from Trapezies Paraelis, Apollakia (left : grave 3, no. 1, upper right : grave 6, nos. 1–2, the rest from grave 7). 1 : 2.

closed-shape jar. The rather coarse fabric is tile-red. The surface is covered in a matt yellow slip. Bands of a brownish-red, lustrous paint.
Max. dimensions : 5.5 × 2.9 cm.

No. 2 (Fig. 81). Fragment of belly from a fine ware, closed-shape jar. Light yellowish, fine-tempered fabric. The surface is covered in a rich yellow, lustrous slip. Bands of dark brown altering to a reddish-brown paint.
Max. dimensions : 3.7 × 2.1 cm.

Grave 7

Three sherds (Fig. 81). Two fine-ware sherds, one of a lid (?), the other probably of an open shape. The third sherd is a coarse-ware side sherd with matt red paint.

Grave 11

Nine sherds were collected from the dromos.

No. 1 (Fig. 82). From closed-shape jar of rather coarse, brownish-grey (2.5 Y 8/4) fabric. Yellow (2.5 Y 8/4), lustrous slip. Decorated in a brown (2.5 Y 5/2), lustrous paint with parallel chevrons (FM 58), at the left framed by a vertical line. Clear wheel traces.
Dimensions : 5.6 × 3.5 cm.

No. 2 (Fig. 82). From upper part of closed-shape jar. Pink (5 YR 7/6), fine-tempered, but thick-walled fabric. Light yellow (10 YR 8/2), matt

Fig. 83. Sherds from Trapezies Paraelis grave 14. (Upper row left : no. 1, right : no. 2. Lower row : no. 3). 1 : 2.

slip. Decorated with horizontal bands and parallel slanting lines in a brown – red if peeled off – matt paint (originally black).
Dimensions : 4.5 × 2.8 cm.

No. 3 (Fig. 82). From a fine ware, closed-shaped jar (stirrup jar?). Pink, fine-tempered fabric. Yellow, burnished slip. Reddish-brown, lustrous paint. Traces of a flower motif (?) on the upper part.
Dimensions : 3.1 × 2.7 cm.

No. 4 (Fig. 82). From upper part of a closed-shape, rather thick-walled jar. Brownish, fine-tempered fabric. Yellow matt slip. Brown paint in horizontal bands and lines.
Dimensions : 9.0 × 7.2 cm.

No. 5 (Fig. 82). Fragment of lower part of band-shaped handle with a conical knob below – from a jar (?). Grey fabric framed by hard yellow zones. Thin yellow slip on outer surface. Black monochrome paint.
Dimensions : 5.6 × 5.3 cm.

No. 6 (Fig. 82). Sherd of pink, coarse fabric with smoothed surface. Incised decoration (Turkish?).
Dimensions : 4.4 × 3.7 cm.
The remaining three sherds were rather insignificant.

Grave 14

No. 1 (Fig. 79, Fig. 83). Rim sherd from large bowl or krater. Pink (2.5 YR 6/6), rather fine fabric. The surface is covered with a yellow (10

YR 8/3), burnished slip. Black paint (black). The rim is covered by a band, 1.9 cm wide on the outside, 1.5 cm on the inside. The outside is decorated with parallel wavy lines, rather debased in style.
Estimated diam. : 24 cm.
Dimensions : 7.0 × 8.0 cm.

No. 2 (Fig. 83). Side sherd from closed-shape jar. Light brown (10 YR 8/3) fabric, pink on surface. Traces of a yellow (10 YR 8/2) slip on outside. Broad band and scale pattern in space-filling grid (FM 70) in a dark red (10 R 6/8) paint.
Dimensions : 5.5 × 4.7 cm.

No. 3 (Fig. 83). Sherd from a fine ware, closed-shape stirrup jar(?). Yellowish-pink fabric. Yellow, burnished slip on the outside. Brownish-red, lustrous paint – parallel, horizontal bands and multiple stem (FM 19).
Dimensions : 3.0 × 2.4 cm.

Grave 16

No. 1 (Fig. 84, Fig. 79). Rim sherd from large bowl or krater. Coarse pink fabric with brown stone inclusions. Smoothed surface.
Dimensions : 3.1 × 3.0 cm.

No. 2 (Fig. 84) is a handle fragment painted brownish-red. Hellenistic.

Grave 19

No. 1 (Fig. 84). Fragment of handle zone of small stirrup jar (evidently having a rather high car-

Fig. 84. Sherds from Trapezies Paraelis graves 16 and 19. (Upper row left : grave 16, no. 1, right : grave 16, no. 2. Lower row : grave 19, no. 1). 1 : 2.

Fig. 85. Sherds from Trapezies Paraelis grave 20. (Upper row left : no. 1, right : no. 2, centre : no. 3. Lower row right : no. 4, above : no. 5). 1 : 2.

ination). Yellow-pink fabric. The surface is covered in a rather matt, yellow slip. Red paint. Encircling bands and lines – a motif of angular multiple stems (FM 19) in the handle zone.
Max dimensions : 7.1 × 3.9 cm.

Grave 20

No. 1 (Fig. 79, Fig. 85). Rim fragment from large

Fig. 86. Various sherds from Trapezies Paraelis (upper row right : no. 1, centre : no. 2. central row centre : no. 3. lower row, left : no. 5, – above no. 5 : no. 6). 1 : 2.

Fig. 87. Trapezies Paraelis, various sherds no. 4. 1 : 2.

open bowl. Greyish-pink (7.5 YR 7/6) fabric. The surface is covered with a grey-yellow (10 YR 8/3), burnished slip. Yellowish-brown (7.5 YR 6/6), thick, matt paint. On the outside two horizontal bands and a broad wavy line pattern. Paint on the rim and slightly down the outside – 0.8 cm in width inside.
Estimated diam. : 24 cm.
Max. dimensions : 10.0 × 8.0 cm.

No. 2 (Fig. 79, Fig. 85). Rim fragment of kylix. Reddish-brown fabric. The surface (inside and out) is covered with a monochrome dark brown (5 YR 3/3), lustrous paint.
Estimated diam. : 16 cm.
Dimensions : 5.0 × 5.8 cm.

No. 3 (Fig. 79, Fig. 85). Rim fragment of an open cup or bowl. Brownish fabric. Smoothed surface. Brown paint on top of rim and a band inside.
Estimated diam. : 14 cm.
Dimensions : 2.9 × 3.0 cm.

No. 4 (Fig. 79, Fig. 85). Bottom fragment with ring-foot of a piriform jug or jar. Pink fabric. Traces of red paint on outside.

No. 5 (Fig. 85). Side fragment of an open-shaped pot. The fabric has a light grey core sandwiched between pink and light brown inside and outside. The inner surface is neatly smoothed, yellow, slightly pink, the outer is covered by a thin, burnished, yellow slip. Decorated with multiple stem, originally black, but badly peeled off. A very fine and rather special ware.
Dimensions : 3.4 × 3.0 cm.
Three side sherds with horizontal bands (Fig. 85).

Fig. 88. The site of Chimaro from the NE – the tomb concerned is by the surveying pole (July 1975).

Various sherds from Trapezies Paraelis

No. 1 (Fig. 79, Fig. 86). Rim sherd of small krater. The fabric is grey and (towards the surface) pink. The inner and outer surfaces are covered in a varying reddish-brown monochrome paint.
Estimated diam. : 14 cm.
Dimensions : 2.9 × 5.1 cm.

No. 2 (Fig. 79, Fig. 86). Rim fragment of a large open krater. Rather coarse fabric with visible stone inclusions. The inner and outer surfaces are smoothed.
Estimated diam. : 30 cm.
Dimensions : 3.7 × 7.2 cm.

No. 3 (Fig. 79, Fig. 86). Rim fragment of a small goblet with splayed rim. Pink fabric, smoothed outer and inner surfaces.
Estimated diam. : 10 cm.

No. 4 (Fig. 87). Fragment with strap handle from the upper part of a large coarse-ware jar (amphora). Pink fabric. The surface is covered in a light yellow slip. Badly peeled brownish-black paint. Horizontal bands and a tassel pattern.
Dimensions : 8.8 × 13.5 cm.

No. 5 (Fig. 86). Sherd of fine-ware, closed-shape jar (stirrup jar). Pink fabric. Surface coated with a yellow, burnished slip. Reddish-brown, lustrous paint. Decoration of horizontal lines and bands surmounted by isolated semicircles and dots.
Dimensions : 4.0 × 2.5 cm.

No. 6 (Fig. 86). Side sherd of brown fabric – closed-shape jar. The surface covered with a very light (almost white) slip. Brown and red lustrous paint – peeled off. Parallel chevrons and tassel frame.

A few other sherds are seen on Fig. 86.

Chimaro, Apollakia

The site is situated on an elevation, a Trapezi, on the northern side of the Apollakia valley – close

74

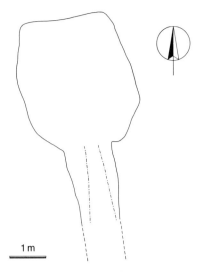

Fig. 89. Mycenaean chamber tomb at Chimaro, outline.

Fig. 91. Surface sherds from around the chamber tomb at Chimaro (upper row right : no. 1, upper row left and centre row right : no. 2). 1 : 2.

to the sea (Fig. 88). It was not mentioned by Kinch, but it was mentioned by Hope Simpson and Lazenby citing Inglieri[10]. The latter authors suggested that the many Mycenaean vases attributed to the Apollakia area "may have come from the cemetery of Chimaro..., but there is no definite proof"[11]. As only one Mycenaean grave was found on the spot in question, this statement can only apply to a very limited number of vases.

The "many vases" might rather have come from "Trapezies Paraelis" and elsewhere. The Mycenaean tomb at Chimaro was localized on the westernmost part of the Trapezi, three or four depressions in the vicinity were evidently not graves, but perhaps holes made by robbers. The grave (fig. 89) was oriented almost directly N (12° towards E) and both dromos and chamber were quite well preserved. As seen on Fig. 90, the side walls of the dromos slope outwards towards the bottom – as was the case at Trapezies Paraelis.

Som sherds were collected from the heaps of soil around the grave:

Catalogue of survey material

No. 1 (Fig. 79, Fig. 91). Rim fragment of small krater. Reddish-yellow (7.5 YR 7/6) fabric. Red-

Fig. 90. The dromos in the chamber tomb at Chimaro (July 1975).

Fig. 92. Conical bowl from Apollakia (Copenhagen inv.no. 5525). 1 : 2.

75

Fig. 93. Stirrup jar from Apollakia (Copenhagen inv.no. 5548). Seen from the side and from above. 1 : 2.

dish-yellow (7.5 YR 7/6), burnished, rich slip on outside – paler on inside. Black paint on the rim. Traces of an unidentified motif to the left.
Estimated diam. : 22 cm.
Dimensions : 4.0 × 5.7 cm.

No. 2 (Fig. 91). Two side sherds from the same closed-shape jar. Reddish-yellow (7.5 YR 7/6) fabric. White (10 YR 8/2) (or very pale brown 8/3), burnished slip on the outside. Brown paint with encircling lines and parts of whorl-shell motifs.

A further four sherds (Fig. 91), one of which has a zigzag pattern in panel, one a diaper grid, and one a stemmed spiral.

Unpublished items having Apollakia as provenance

The following items having Apollakia as their provenance were purchased by members of the expedition. All were acquired in the city of Rhodes in 1903.

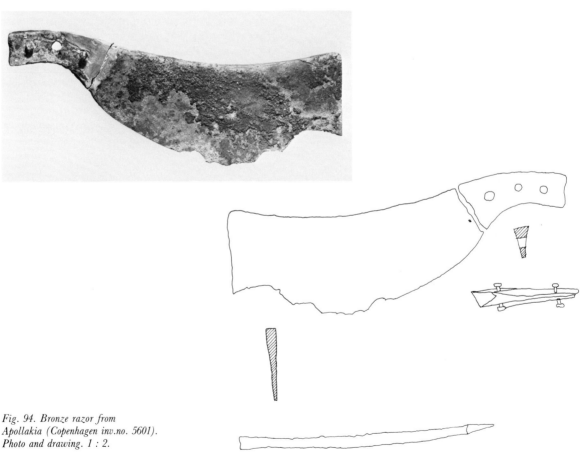

Fig. 94. Bronze razor from Apollakia (Copenhagen inv.no. 5601). Photo and drawing. 1 : 2.

76

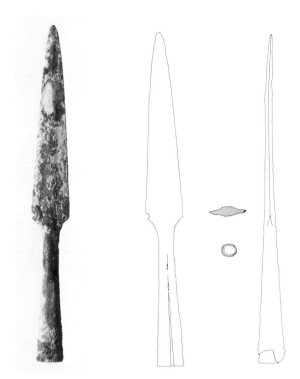

Fig. 95. Spearhead from Apollakia (Copenhagen inv.no. 5602). 1 : 4.

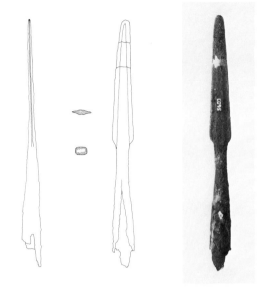

Fig. 96. Spearhead from Apollakia (Copenhagen inv.no. 5603). 1 : 4.

Copenhagen inv.no. 5525 (Figs 92 and 120). Conical, handleless cup with convex-concave profile. Low, pronounced, flat base. Preserved intact. Reddish-yellow fabric (7.5 YR 7/6). Faint slip or just smoothing in the same colour.
H. : 7.5 cm.
D. : 12.0 cm.

Copenhagen inv.no. 5548 (Figs. 93 and 116). Small depressed globular stirrup jar (FS 171). Low ring-foot. Very pale brown (10 YR 7/4), finely tempered fabric. White (2.5 Y 8/2) lustrous slip. The paint was originally black and lustrous, but is now almost totally peeled off. Decorated in the handle zone with Mycenaean III flowers (FM 18) – the anther is almost arrow-shaped. Several parallel lines on the body. Concentric circles on the disc plate.
H. : 9.1 cm.
W. : 8.6 cm.

Copenhagen inv.no. 5601 (Fig. 94). Bronze razor ("Hiebmesser") having a simple square handle with nail holes – two nails preserved (however, all three nails were extant earlier). Part of the blade missing and the handle repaired.
L. : 18.5 cm.
Max. W. (as preserved) : 5.4 cm.

Copenhagen inv.no. 5602 (Fig. 95). Bronze spearhead. Repair on the blade and a small part of the edge missing, otherwise completely preserved – but badly corroded. The slashed socket is facetted, with eight facets (octagonal) and two oppositely placed fastening holes, 1.7 cm from the end. The triangular blade is thickened at the centre.
L. : 35.2 cm.
Max. W. at blade : 4.1 cm.
Max. W. at the socket : 2.9 cm.

Copenhagen inv.no. 5603 (Fig. 96). Bronze spearhead. Cut at the lower part of the socket and repaired at the blade and the socket. The socket is almost circular and slashed, evidently the cut runs through the centre of the oppositely placed fastening holes. The lanceolate blade has an amygdaloid section.
L. as preserved : 27.1 cm.
Max. W. of blade : 2.4 cm.
Max W. of the socket : 2.4 cm.

A3 The Kattavia area

Sto Granto Kattavia

On July 27th, 1908 – after finishing in Vroulia – Kinch started excavations at a place called Sto Granto, "immediately to the N of Kattavia, where the inhabitants had been excavating previously".

The site was not definitely identified during the 1975 survey but, as pointed out by R. Hope Simpson and J. F. Lazenby, the artificially made depressions and smaller cavities in the slope between the chapel of Agh. Minas and Kattavia might well represent Mycenaean graves[12]. This slope is still called Granto today – but only very few and very insignificant sherds were found on the slope itself. At the very top, just south of the chapel of Agh. Minas, however, quite a number of sherds was found. Among these, sherds of the early Archaic period and probably Mycenaean coarse-ware sherds could be identified. As pointed out by Hope Simpson and Lazenby, a Mycenaean settlement might have existed on the spur.

The location of the site was not given exactly in Kinch's diary, but many sherds "of ordinary Mycenaean vases of the latest style" were evidently scattered on the surface.

The most important grave excavated by Kinch was No. 1, which was, however, partly washed away by rain water (Fig. 97). The dromos lay SSE (at 145° on a 360° scale), dimensions 1.02 × 3.00 m – the walls were almost vertical. The stomion was closed by large stones (Fig. 97, c). As seen on the sketch (Fig. 97, b), the pottery lay just inside the door to the right and in the north-eastern corner. In the left half of the grave (viewed from the entrance) was a skull, and bones lay scattered from the skull and up into a cavity cut in the soft rock to the left of the entrance.

Further finds in this area were one steatite seal stone (No. 20, not identified) and one bead (No. 21). Kinch supposed the skeleton to have been placed on its right side with straight torso and heavily contracted legs (lying in the cavity).

Another Mycenaean tomb, No. 2, was excavated under the direction of Wace and Thompson :

Dimensions :
Dromos + stomion : 3.75 m.
Dromos, width at door : 0.86–0.98 m.
Chamber : 1.35 (N-S) × 1.23 (E-W).

The chamber was said to be rectangular.

No finds were reported from this grave and only a very sketchy drawing remains. In the listing of items forwarded to Constantinople four vases were reported, however, to have been found in grave 2 (not identified).

Grave 3 was Mycenaean, but a Hellenistic grave had disturbed the original grave. In the list of items sent to Constantinople, three kylikes (?) were said to have been found in grave 3 (not identified.).

Catalogue of grave goods

Grave 1

1. From Kinch's file : "Amphore à trois anses. En beaucoup de fragments (h.c. : 0.38 m)". Not identified.
2. From Kinch's file : Coupe sans décor. Bien conservées (H. 0.75 m, Diam. 0.13 m)". Not identified. (One-handled cup, horizontal handle).

3. (Ist. inv.no. 4640). (Fig. 98, Fig. 117).
Large piriform jar with three vertical handles, with central bead and two finger impressions at the transition to the body (FS 35). Much restored with gypsum. Rather light red fabric. The surface covered in a reddish-yellow slip. Brown/black paint. Where the paint has peeled off, the

78

*Fig. 97. Sto Granto, grave 1.
From Kinch's sketchbook,
a : chamber with stomion and
dromos – the numbers refer
to the outline,
b : offerings and bones
recorded in the chamber,
c : the filling of the stomion.*

Fig. 98. Piriform jar 1,3 (Ist. inv.no. 4640) from Granto grave 1. 1 : 4.

decoration is visible as a depression in the slip. Foot and stem painted. Three bands encircle the lower part of the belly and three the upper part, below the handle zone. Between the handles are three running spiral ornaments (FM 46). The

handle is painted on the outside and a band surrounds it. Neck painted. The broad collar rim is decorated on top with varying U-patterns (FM 45,4). The paint continues down the inner surface of the neck.
Max. H. : 35.8 cm.
Max. W. : 29.1 cm.

4. From Kinch's file : "Coupe à pied et à deux (?) anses, sans décor, en fragments" (h. ?). Not identified. (Low-stemmed kylix 11 cm H).

5. From Kinch's file : "Coupe à pied haut, sans décor, en fragments (H. 19.5 cm)". Not identified.

6. (Ist. inv.no. 4623). (Fig. 99, Fig. 118).
Piriform, spouted jug with two handles preserved and ring-foot. The handle opposite the spout is missing (but traces where it joined the body are clearly seen). Several fragments are missing. Faint yellow slip on surface. Decorated with a rather matt varying brownish/black paint. Foot and stem painted. The body is decorated with three horizontal zones consisting of broader bands framing thinner lines. In the handle zone there is an area with a foliate band pattern (FM 64,19). Crossing wavy lines are painted on the outside of the handle, there is a band round the root of the handle, and the spout is painted. Clear wheel traces under the bottom.
Max. H. : 15.5 cm.
Max. W. : 10.4 cm.

7. (Ist. inv.no. 4641) (Fig. 100, Fig. 117).
Large piriform jar with three vertical strap handles with central bead and two grooves at the transition to the body, and low ring-foot. Parts of the rim and foot repaired with gypsum. Red fabric. The surface is covered in a yellowish-red

Fig. 99. Piriform, spouted jug 1,6 (Ist. inv.no. 4623) from Granto grave 1. 1 : 2.

slip. Decorated with black/brown varying with yellow-red lustrous paint. Paint on stem and foot. Two zones of three bands each encircle the lower part of the body and the upper part beneath the handle zone. Between the handles are three running spirals (FM 46,43) of seven turns. The handles are painted on the outside and there is a broad band round them. The zone between the handles and the neck is decorated with encircling, parallel lines. The neck is monochrome and the top of the outwards sloping, splayed collar rim has a pattern of foliate bands (FM 64,19).
Max. H. : 39.5 cm.
Max. W. : 30.7 cm.

8. From Kinch's file : "Coupe à pied haut, sans décor, en fragments" (H. 19.5 cm)". Not identified. (Kylix).

9. From Kinch's file : "Coupe à deux anses et à embouchure. Décorée – en fragments (H. : ?)". Not identified. (Kylix).

10. From Kinch's file : "Marmite à trois pieds et à anse. Un des pieds manque. Fragmenté". Not identified.

11. (Copenh. inv.no. 12352) (Fig. 101).

Truncated conical bead in steatite. H. : 1.3 cm, W. : 2.3 cm.

12. (Ist. inv.no. 4622) (Fig. 102, Fig. 116).
Depressed globular stirrup jar on a very low hollowed base (FS 171). The spout is much fragmented. Reddish fabric. The surface is covered with a thin light yellow slip. Decoration in shimmering red to black lustrous colours. The body is decorated with encircling lines and bands. The handle zone is decorated with multiple stem and tongue pattern (FM 19) with five to seven semi-

Fig. 101. Bead of steatite 1,11 (Copenhagen inv.no. 12352) and spindle whorl in lead 1,14 (Copenhagen inv.no. 12353) from Granto grave 1. 1 : 1.

Fig. 102. Stirrup jar 1,12 (Ist. inv.no. 4622) from Granto grave 1. Seen from the side and from above. 1 : 2.

circles. Bands surround the roots of the spout and the false neck. The strap handles are painted outside and on the top plate is a painted circle with a circular recess at the centre.
Max. H. : 12.7 cm.
Max. W. : 13.2 cm.

13. (Ist. inv.no. 4619) (Fig. 103, Fig. 116).
Conical, piriform stirrup jar with splayed hollowed base (FS 166). A few fragments missing

from the spout, otherwise complete. Red fabric. The surface is covered with a rich yellow slip. Lustrous red paint altering to brown/black in a few places. Foot and stem painted. The body is decorated with four encircling bands. The handle zone is decorated with multiple stem and tongue pattern (FM 19,21) and an accessorial motif. Paint on the outside of the strap handles – a triangle left free at the top. The spout is painted round the root, mouth and inside the

Fig. 103. Stirrup jar 1,13 (Ist. inv.no. 4619) from Granto grave 1. Seen from the side and from above. 1 : 2.

mouth. The false neck has a ring band round the root, three painted concentric circles, and a central dot on the top plate.

Max. H. : 18.5 cm.
Max. W. : 14.9 cm.

14. (Copenh. inv.no. 12353) (Fig. 101).
Sfondyli of lead. H. : 1.1 cm, W. : 1.7 cm

15. (Ist.inv.no. 4620) (Fig. 104, Fig. 116).
Conical, piriform stirrup jar with ring-foot

Fig. 106. Flat cup no. 1,19 (Ist. inv.no. 4623) from Granto grave 1. 1 : 2.

(torus-disc base) (FS 166). Preserved intact. Red-brown fabric. The surface is covered in a thin brown-yellow slip. Black, matt, badly peeled paint. Foot and stem painted. The body is decorated with four encircling zones consisting of parallel lines framed by broader bands. Decoration in the handle zone of parallel chevrons (FM 58) and one U (FM 45). The strap handles are decorated with cross bands. Four concentric circles are painted on the top plate; the neck and spout have separated circle bands at the root.
Max. H. : 20.8 cm.
Max. W. : 16.5 cm.

16. From Kinch's file : "Lampe, sans anses. Sans décoration" (h. 7 cm)". Not identified. Undecorated cup without handles.

17. From Kinch's file : "Coupe à l'anse, sans décor. Bien conservées (H. 6.5 cm, Diam. : 12.5 cm)". Not identified. (One-handled cup as no. 2).

18. (Ist. inv.no. 4621) (Fig. 105, Fig. 116). Piriform stirrup jar with ring-foot (torus disc) (FS 166). Fragments of foot and belly missing. Red-brown fabric. Yellow slip with a red tinge on surface. Decoration in varying matt brown/red paint. Base and stem painted. The body is decorated with four horizontal, encircling zones of parallel thin lines framed by broader bands. Parallel chevrons (FM 58) and one U-pattern (FM 45) in the handle zone. The strap handles are painted along the edge and have three sloping cross bands. The spout has a band at the root and round the mouth. Another oval band around the false neck touches the band round the spout. Five concentric circles on the top plate.
Max. H. : 16.1 cm.
Max W. : 11.9 cm.

19. (Ist. inv.no. 4632) (Fig. 106, Fig. 120). Flat cup with one strap handle and ring-foot. A few fragments missing from the rim. Grey, red-tinged fabric. Dark yellow slip inside and out. Decorated in red and brown-red. Decoration inside the bottom of eight thin concentric (around the centre) lines framed by broader band circles. Foliate band motifs (FM 64,19) outside in the handle zone. The rim is painted on the upper side with triangular area left free where the handle joins the cup.
Max. H. (above handle) : 5.0 cm.
Max. W. : 14.3 cm.

20. From Kinch's file : "Gem of steatite". Not identified.

21. From Kinch's file : "Flat bead with string hole". Not identified.

Grave 2 (no items identified).
1. Lampe sans anses et sans décoration. Bien conservée. h. 0.075 m.

2. Petit vase à anse et embouch. Litua. (?) et l'embouche manquant.

3. Amphore à trois anses (comme tombeau 1,1). En beaucoup de fragments. Décoration a imbrications sur l'épaule du vase. (h. : ?).

4. Plusieurs fragments de vases pas encore lavés et très degradés.

Granto Grave 3 (no items were identified).
1. Coupe à pied, sans décoration. En fragments.

2.   do.   noir   do.

3.   do.   noir   do.

(Grave 4 was Hellenistic).

Ta Tzingani, Kattavia

On August 1st, 1908, Kinch excavated a Mycenaean tomb at a place called τα Τζιγγάνι. Evidently, the site was very close to στο Γραντο – but the exact position was not given. During the 1975 survey the inhabitants of Kattavia informed us that it was the area immediately to the East of the Granto slope that was called τα Τζιγγάνι. The grave *a* was partly emptied by the Kattavians, but at the bottom there were a few bones, a bronze knife, two undecorated kylikes, one undecorated bowl and fragments of a stirrup jar. The grave is depicted on Fig. 107. It was furthermore reported that a basket had been found by the peasants, but it had disintegrated when brought home. The grave was not further described by Kinch.

84

Fig. 107. Ta Tzingani (Kattavia) grave a (from Kinch's sketch-book). N to the right.

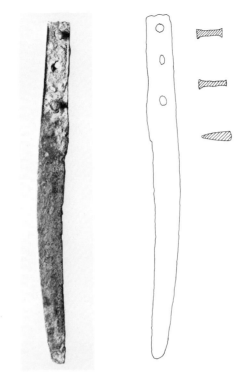

Fig. 108. One-edged knife no. 1 from the chamber tomb at Ta Tzingani (Copenhagen inv.no. 7700). Photo and drawing. 1 : 2.

Grave goods in grave *a* (the numbers refer to the plan Fig. 107).

1. (Copenh. inv.no. 7700) (Fig. 108). Bronze knife with evenly curved, thickened back and curved edge. The handle zone, which has three nail-holes (only two nails are preserved), has very short flanges. The blade has evidently been sharpened.
The nails are thickened at the ends.
L. : 18.3 cm.
L. of handle : 5.4 cm.
L. of nails : 1.4 cm (lower nail) and 1.3 cm (upper nail).
W. at handle : 1.5 cm (widening towards the blade).

2. (from Kinch's file) : Fragmentarily preserved stirrup jar.

3. (from Kinch's file) : Undecorated bowl (evidently a kylix).

4. (from Kinch's file) : Undecorated bowl (evidently a kylix).

5. (from Kinch's file) : Fragment of undecorated bowl.

Other fragments were found (of a large vase, etc.).

Other items having Kattavia as provenance

Copenh. inv.no. 7701 (Fig. 109). Fish hook of bronze with barb. The tang is flat (hammered ?) while the wire for the hook has a circular section.
L. : 4.5 cm.

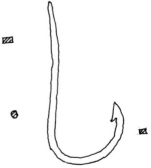

Fig. 109. Fish hook (Copenhagen inv.no. 7701) from Mycenaean grave at Kattavia. 1 : 1.

Fig. 110. Two necklaces from Kattavia (Copenhagen inv.nos. 7702 and 7703). 1 : 2.

Provenance : From a Mycenaean tomb at Kattavia.
Copenhagen inv.no. 7702–7703 (Fig. 110).

Inv.no. 7702 is a collection of carnelian beads :
– 27 small spherical beads (average L. : 0.5 cm)[13].
– 1 cylindrical (L. : 1.4 cm)[14].
– 9 amygdaloid, facetted beads (L. : between 1.5 and 2.5 cm)[15]. Four show longitudinal incised lines.

Inv.no. 7703 is a collection of various beads :
– 53 small, discoid, green faience beads (Fig. 110), 8 brown and two yellow/white.
– 7 angular, amygdaloid beads of steatite (shape and material as in Fig. 110), one showing an incised pattern of parallel chevrons on the flanges, one having longitudinal incised lines on one flange.
– 12 smaller and larger spherical and flattened spherical beads in stone, clay, glass-paste and faience. The glass-paste bead (in the centre of Fig. 110) shows incised (?) lines in the longitudinal axes.
– 3 blue faience beads shaped like a "grain of wheat"[16] (also Fig. 63).
– 1 grooved, flattened. spherical bead.
– 1 tubular faience bead.
– 2 amygdaloid carnelian beads. One is facetted (like 7702).
– 2 lentoid, white glass-paste beads. One shows an incised pattern of a stylized tree (parallel chevrons).
– and one small fragmented scarab in composite paste, blue in colour.

A4 Unpublished items having Rhodes as provenance

Copenh. inv.no. 7566 (Fig. 111) (from Kinch's private collection). Rim sherd of kylix. Reddish-yellow (7.5 YR 6/6), finely tempered fabric. Surface coated with a very pale brown (10 YR 8/4), fine, slightly burnished slip. A red band (2.5 YR 5/6) covers the rim – 1.0 cm wide on the outside, 0.5 cm inside. A horizontal zone (L. : 4.1 cm) beneath the rim band contains a rather peculiar pattern (red paint : 2.5, 5/8) – similar to the tricurved arch (FM 62), or linked whorl-shell, with the top cut off – connected to parallel, curved lines with fringes. Four parallel, horizontal bands are preserved of the lower frame of the zone.

H. : 5.6 cm.
W. : 11.5 cm.
Estim. diam. : 15 cm.
Provenance : Rhodes.

Copenh. inv.no. 7704 (Fig. 112). Carnelian

Fig. 113. Kylix having Rhodes as provenance (Copenhagen inv.no. 12364). 1 : 2.

Fig. 111. Rim sherd of deep bowl from Rhodes (Copenhagen inv.no. 7566). 1 : 2.

Fig. 112. A carnelian bead from Mallona and two gold rosettes having Rhodes as provenance. (Copenhagen inv.no. 7704 and 7706). 1 : 1.

bead, amygdaloid with incised line in the centre of the longitudinal direction. String hole through centre[17].

L. : 2.3 cm.
W. : 1.8 cm.
H. : 0.9 cm.
Provenance : Malona.

Copenhagen inv.no. 7706 (Fig. 112). Two circular sheets of gold foil with rosette pattern in relief, the rosette having eight petals. Two holes around the central circle.

D. : 1.5 cm.
Provenance : Rhodes (?).

Copenhagen inv.no. 12364 (Figs. 113 and 121). Bowl and part of stem of kylix. Very pale brown (10 YR 7/4), finely tempered fabric. The surface is covered by a thin, slightly burnished, very pale brown (10 YR 8/4) slip. Black or very dark grey

Fig. 114. Stirrup jar having Rhodes as provenance (Copenhagen inv.no. 12501). Seen from the side and from above. 1 : 2.

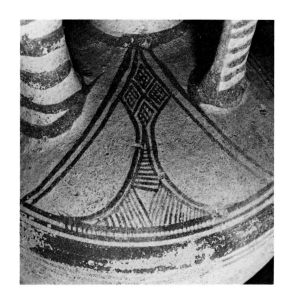

Fig. 115. Stirrup jar having provenance "Lindos SW above town, 21/4–14". Yaltos. (Copenhagen inv.no. 12502), 1 : 5.

lustrous paint. Band on top of rim, sloping whorl-shell (FM 23) and sea anemone (FM 27, 23), one double (FM 27, 25). Horizontal, parallel lines below the handle zone. Rings around the stem.
Preserved H. : 11.5 cm.
D. : 13.7 cm.
Provenance : Rhodes.

Copenh. inv.no. 12501 (Figs. 114 and 116). Biconical stirrup jar with torus-disc base and a bulb around the base of the false neck, a flat disc on top of the false neck. Except for a hole in the belly the piece is totally intact. Yellowish-red fabric (5 YR 5/6), coarsely tempered with mainly white (chalk) inclusions, which are also seen on the surface. The surface has a matt, white (10 YR 8/2) slip. Matt, black (very dark grey) paint. There is a broad band of paint on the base and two parallel bands above. A horizontal wavy line encircles the false neck, and seven groups of three vertical wavy lines (FM 53, 39) decorate the handle zone, being terminated below by three parallel, encircling bands. Three bands around the false neck, paint on the mouth

of the cylindrical spout, a band on the centre and around the base of the spout. Parallel strokes on the handles and a cross (FM 17,36 – from Salamis) on the top of the false neck.
H. : 26.4 cm.
Max. W. (belly) : 20.3 cm.
Provenance : Rhodes.

Copenh. inv.no. 12502 (Figs. 115 and 116). Ovoid-conical (in fact egg-shaped) stirrup jar with torus-disc base, funnel-shaped high spout, two flat strap-handles and a broad, flat disc with a coned centre and an air hole. Totally preserved. Light brown (7.5 YR 6/4) coarse fabric with brown and a few white stone inclusions. The surface is covered by a white (10 YR 8/2) matt slip. Decoration in black or very dark brown, matt paint. The decoration in the handle zone is four triangular panels framed by double lines (FM 71) :

1) to the right of the spout there is a dense horizontal zigzag pattern on the lower part, detached, vertical, parallel chevrons on the upper.

2) to the left of the spout is an inscribed triangle with painted decoration consisting of a rhomboid figure with a central cross separating four cross-hatched lozenges. The corners of the triangle are filled with parallel lines. The pattern continues with vertical, parallel lines in the upper band of the lower frame.

The two patterns on the rear side are separated by two vertical, parallel lines :

3) the pattern to the right is the only one that has a concave filling with scale pattern (FM 70).

4) the pattern to the left. The large triangle is divided into smaller straight-sided triangles by straight lines. Some of the smaller triangles have angles filled with parallel straight lines – constituting a geometric pattern.

The lower frame of the handle zone decoration consists of a broad band (2 cm) surrounded by two double lines. Two parallel, encircling bands are painted on the lower part of the belly. A band is painted around the base and the rim of the spout, and four horizontal lines are painted on the front and on the sides of the spout (the back is left free). Parallel, horizontal lines on the handles and a (left-turned) spiral on the disc.

H. : 39.0 cm.

W. : 27.8 cm.

Provenance : The jar was purchased by Kinch at Lindos during his visit in 1913–14. The provenance is stated as "Lindos SW above town, 21/1–1914". Kinch's diary relates that the man ("Christos") selling the jar supposed that it had been found in a place called Yaltos, south of Lindos. However, Kinch viewed this statement with some scepticism.

Fig. 116.

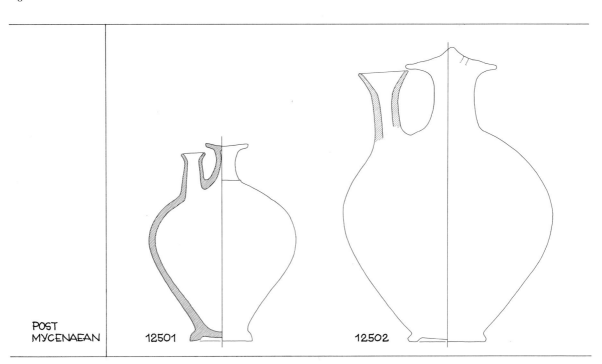

POST MYCENAEAN

12501

12502

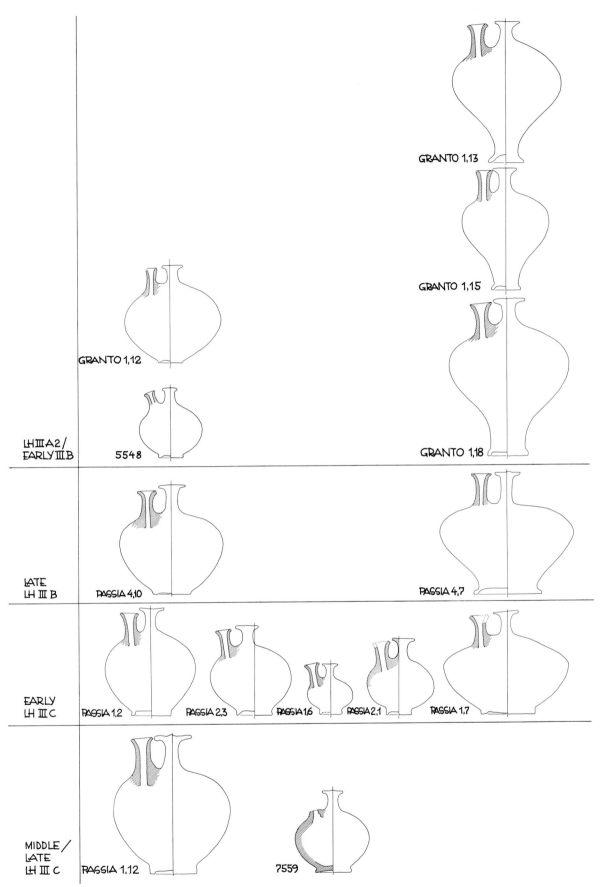

LH III A2/
EARLY III B

GRANTO 1,12

5548

GRANTO 1,13

GRANTO 1,15

GRANTO 1,18

LATE
LH III B

PASSIA 4,10

PASSIA 4,7

EARLY
LH III C

PASSIA 1,2   PASSIA 2,3   PASSIA 1,6   PASSIA 2,1   PASSIA 1,7

MIDDLE/
LATE
LH III C

PASSIA 1,12

7559

Fig. 116. Sections of stirrup jars in chronological sequence. 1 : 5.

91

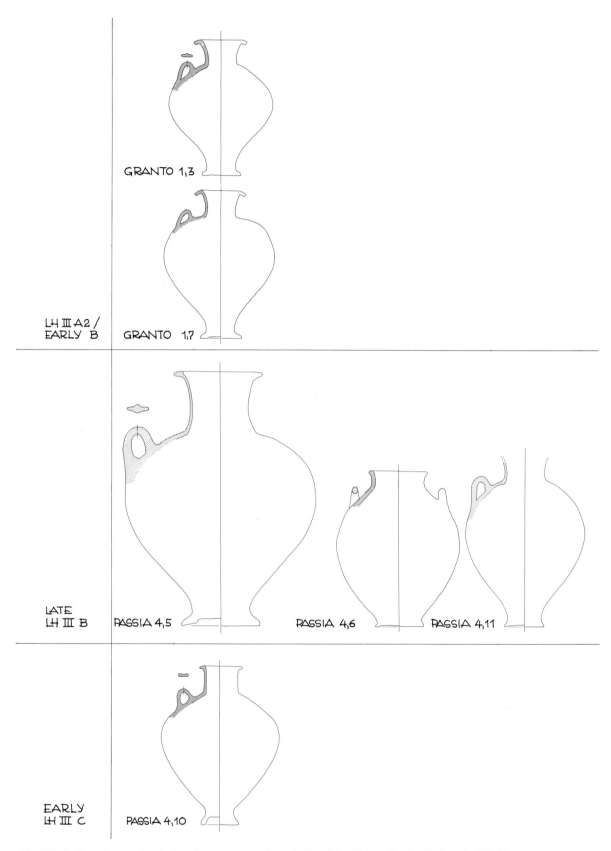

GRANTO 1,3

GRANTO 1,7

LH III A2 / EARLY B

LATE LH III B

PASSIA 4,5

PASSIA 4,6

PASSIA 4,11

EARLY LH III C

PASSIA 4,10

Fig. 117. Sections of storage jars in chronological sequence. Scales 1 : 5 and 1 : 10 (note that Passia 4,10 should be Passia 1,10).

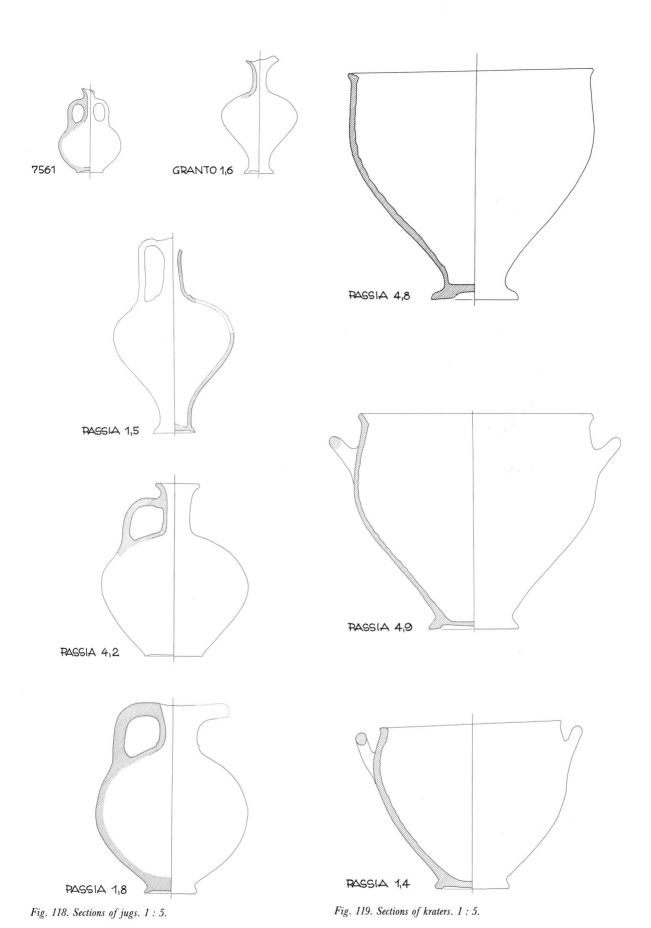

7561

GRANTO 1,6

PASSIA 1,5

PASSIA 4,2

PASSIA 1,8

PASSIA 4,8

PASSIA 4,9

PASSIA 1,4

Fig. 118. Sections of jugs. 1 : 5.

Fig. 119. Sections of kraters. 1 : 5.

93

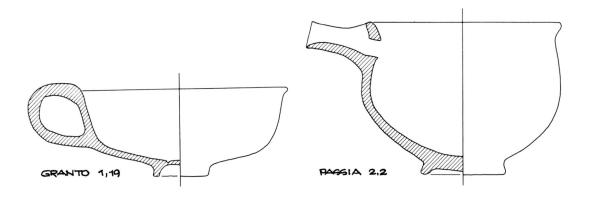

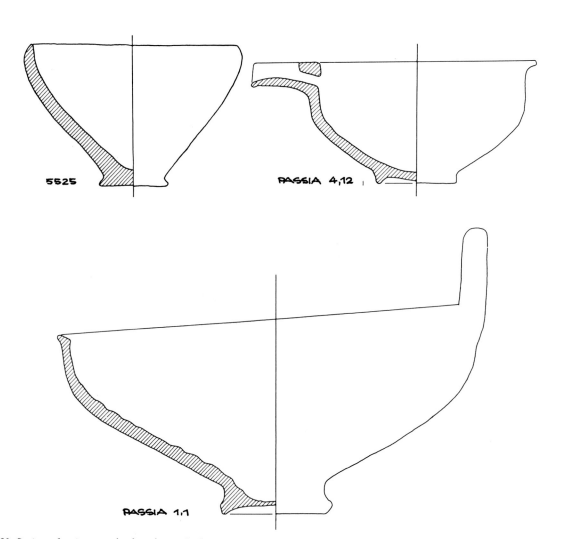

Fig. 120. Sections of various open bowls and cups. 1 : 2.

94

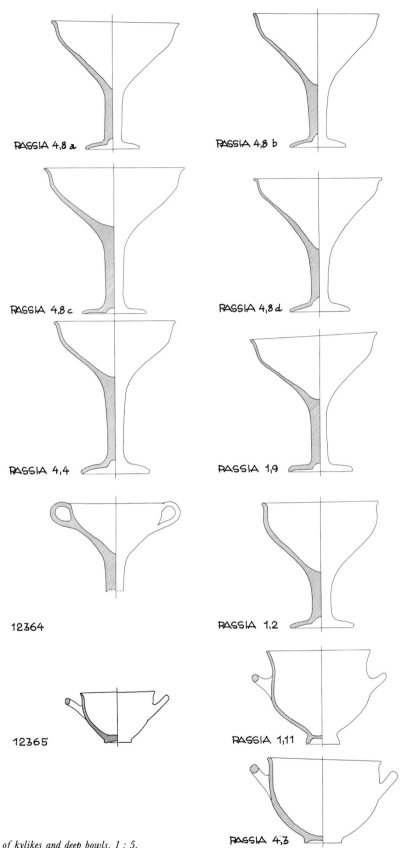

RASSIA 4,8 a

RASSIA 4,8 b

RASSIA 4,8 c

RASSIA 4,8 d

RASSIA 4,4

RASSIA 1,9

12364

RASSIA 1,2

12365

RASSIA 1,11

RASSIA 4,3

Fig. 121. Sections of kylikes and deep bowls. 1 : 5.

B. Chronology and discussion

The Cemetery of Passia

Grave 1
Comments

Four individuals were evidently interred in this grave. One was in the centre, at the bottom of the grave. Close by, but at a higher level, the bones of another body were found. A skull is depicted on the plan but its presence was not explicitly stated in the text. Finally, bones of two bodies lay in the SW corner.

From a chronological point of view, the statement that sherds from pottery found as grave goods were found outside the stomion is of interest. Unfortunately, we are not informed from which vases these sherds originated. Consequently it can be estimated that the latest burial should be that close to the pots 11–13, while the concentration in the SW corner should represent at least two chronological phases. No material could be attributed to the skull at the bottom of the grave in the centre, but it seems reasonable to suggest that even this is included in the concentration in the SW corner. The sherds in the dromos might originate from a cleaning of the grave in order to make room for a new body – even if grave goods from earlier burials were evidently deposited in the SW corner.

1,1. Shallow, angular bowls of this type with handle on rim are rather unusual in published Mycenaean material. Furumark lists one example under FS 297, a piece said to be from Lachania in southern Rhodes[18]. The bowl from Lachania does have a similar angular section; it has flatter handles and linear decoration. Another similar piece was excavated by I. Zervoudaki at Armenokhori in Astypalia. The shape of this piece is close to that of ours, and there is decoration consisting of parallel, horizontal wavy lines in a panel. The two graves in question contain pottery from LH IIIA 1 to middle LH IIIC with early and late IIIA, early and late IIIB and early/middle IIIC represented[19]. 121 vases were found in the two graves and only a few are depicted[20]. Further one bowl of exactly the same shape and decoration with parallel, slanting lines in the vertical zone below the rim was found in Astypalia (now in the Rhodes museum) Thanks to the triangular chevron pattern in the handle-zone of the bowl 1,1, a dating in IIIC should be quite safe (but the pattern is quite similar, however, in LM IIIB). Furthermore the continuation of the decoration zone between the handles is unusual in Mycenaean pottery, but is also seen on the bowl from Armenokhori in Astypalia. The same feature is furthermore seen on a shallow bowl from Crete with vertical handles on the rim, decorated with a simple version of the foliate band (FM 64,20)[21]. The shape might have developed from late LH IIIB 1 bowls as found in Mycenae[22]. With respect to shape some of the unpainted bowls of Troy VIIa are actually very closely related[23].

1,2. The stirrup jars FS 175 and 176 were recently treated by Mee, who – in accordance with Furumark – considers FS 176 to be far the most usual IIIC type of stirrup jar in the Ialysos cemeteries[24]. Semicircles in a triangular patch (FM 42,21) are found on FS 176 in *Ialysos* OT 13[25], and *Ialysos* NT 17 (2706)[26]. Another close parallel with respect to shape and decoration is no. 145 from Perati Grave 9[27]. The pattern is also seen on a IIIC : 1 amphoriskos from Tiryns, Unterburg[28]. The semicircle pattern seems rather to be executed as superimposed zigzag lines, the triangles ending in a semicircle – features considered by Furumark to be characteristic of the early "IIIC : 1 period"[29]. Jar 1,2 should be dated early in the IIIC period.

1,3. The kylix should be safely dated within the LH IIIA 2 period. Rather similar pieces have

96

been found in other parts of Rhodes including the Vati Area[30]. The octopus design is akin to the pattern on a jug from the IIIA 2 grave, *Ialysos* NT 28[31]. C. Mee considers that the Ialysos FS 267 kylikes were probably imported from the Mainland. "The only possible exceptions are the octopus kylikes for the extensive use of white paint might be considered a characteristic of Rhodes although Mainland examples do exist"[32].

*1,4.*The shape of the bell-krater (FS 281/282) is most unusual on Rhodes, but very common on the Mainland and, not least, on Cyprus. One main difference between 281 and 282 seems to be that the handles on the latter are usually placed on the broadest part of the vase, on the former the handles are placed higher up (note the difference between Passia 1,4 and Passia 4,9 (FS 281)). Kraters are known in the settlement material from Mycenae, but it is said that the development is not clear[33]. In the new excavations at Tiryns kraters occur from IIIB 2 at least; however, in IIIB 2/IIIC früh, the shape is evidently not very common, and none of the published sections and sherds are close to ours. In the later phases the shape takes other directions. With respect to the shape and band decoration, there is a close parallel from the Citadel house at Mycenae[34]. This krater should be considered LH IIIC (early)[35]. Furumark considered the pattern FM 53,15 to be a LH IIIC early type. (Note that the IIIC variant can hardly be distinguished from the IIIA 2). A very similar elaboration of the pattern is seen on a jug from *Ialysos* NT 61 (12.606). The grave was included in Furumark's "IIIC : 1b" period[36]. Other cases of the pattern : Tiryns[37], Pilona, Rhodes[38], Seraglio Kos[39]. I suggest a dating in the early IIIC period for the krater 1,4.

1,5. The piriform jug type FS 151 is very common in Rhodes[40]. Dating IIIA 2 (late)[41].

1,6. Like stirrup jar 2,1, this piece should be counted among Furumark's FS 171. However, it differs from most of the specimens included in the group by being extraordinarily small and having an extremely simple band decoration – without the filling of thin lines. The sea anemone motif (FM 27) is found in the Argolid from LH IIIA 1 onwards[42], and it is not unusual on Rhodes[43]. I propose a dating for this piece in the LH IIIC period, similar, for instance, to catalogue No. 685 from Perati grave 84 which is of almost the same shape and similar decoration[44]. An unpublished IIIC stirrup jar in the National Mu-

Fig. 122. Stirrup jar purchased in Italy (Copenhagen inv.no. 8696). Seen from the side and from above. 1 : 2.

seum, Copenhagen, should probably be reckoned to belong to the same group, but it is without ring-base and probably somewhat later (Fig. 122)[45]. For the spiral see Eleona[46]. The decoration seems to point towards Crete[47].

1,7. The shape FS 180 was considered a IIIB type by Furumark, while the heavier type 181 should be dated within the IIIC period. I suspect, however, that the boundary is rather vague and that the stirrup jar 1,7 should be dated within the IIIC period (early). The pattern FM 42,33 joining semicircles in a "triangular patch" framed by a line, is probably a characteristic IIIC type of decoration[48]. Joining semicircles in a space-filling grid are not usual in handle zones of stirrup jars. A rather good parallel comes from Vati, Rhodes[49]. A similar pattern on a stirrup jar from Klauss in Achaea was published by Th. Papadopoulos[50].
In Tarsus rather similar patterns are found in stirrup jar handle zones in IIIC contexts[51]. The pattern is also found in IIIC contexts in Perati[52], and in a IIIC context in Langada, Kos[53]. On the present evidence I should propose a date in early IIIC.

1,8. The jug should be put in a group of mainly South Rhodian vases decorated with geometric patterns such as parallel chevrons, parallel zigzags and triangle motif. This group is represented by three pieces in the present grave (1,1–1,8 and 1,10). Further jugs from this group are found in the National Museum, Copenhagen, two with indicated provenance "The Island of Rhodes",[54], one with provenance Apollakia, Rhodes[55]. Rather similar are a further two jugs from Apollakia, Rhodes[56]. With respect to chronology, there was some confusion in Furumark's treatment. In *MP*, Furumark dated all five Copenhagen jugs in his LH IIIC : C1 (late), while one jug in Istanbul, which must necessarily be our *1,8*, was dated in his LH III : Ia[57]. In *Furumark IIIC* the jug *CVA* DK, 44, 5 was dated to LH IIIC : 1b[58]. However, later in the same article[59], the jugs *CVA* DK, 44, 5–6 were dated to his IIIC : 1c period. C. Mee dated *CVA* DK, 44, 3 to LH IIIC[60,] while 44, 4–5 were dated LH IIIB. Regarding the various motifs, the zigzag appeared already in LH IIIA 2 (for instance, on a pilgrim flask from *Ialysos* NT 28 : 7[61] and a rhyton said to be from Kalavarda, Rhodes[62]). The triangular motif is probably IIIC (see supra 1,1), while the flower pattern must be a local, degenerated variation of an original IIIA motif. According to Furumark, "pendant curves attached to handle bases" are typically "Granary Style"[63]. The triangular solid motif on the spout is found on the jug *CVA* DK, Pl. 44,3. A fragment from a jug identical to 1,8 is from Lachania, Southern Rhodes[64]. The spout on the jug from Lachania is preserved and upturned. This was undoubtedly also the shape of the spout on Passia 1,8 (which is thus wrongly reconstructed). The triangular pattern and the flower are not found on the Lachania piece, the band around spout and handle, however, run similarly. This piece was dated to IIIC 1 by C. Mee[65]. Proposed dating : early LH IIIC.

1,9. The unpainted kylix is hard to date more precisely. However, it is important to note that the type is still in use in the earlier part of LH IIIC[66].

1,10. Furumark considered the ovoid biconical jar FS 38 to be a IIIC 1 type. Among the jars mentioned, that from *Ialysos* NT 17 : 14 – which is closest to ours – was placed in IIIC : 1 late. The jar should be placed in the same group as nos. 1,1 and 1,8 (supra). Biconical, three-handled jars FS 37–38 were found in some of the graves at Eleona and Langada, Kos. With respect to the general shape of the body and the cylinder neck, a piece from the IIIC grave 20 at Eleona is rather similar[67]. Another from grave 60[68] probably represents a slightly earlier stage of the type. Two biconical FS 38, three-handled jars are in the National Museum, Copenhagen[69]. Proposed dating : LH IIIC (early).

1,11. An astonishingly close parallel was found in *Ialysos* NT 17 : 55[70]. Every detail of the two bowls is similar – thus they both show the same unpainted circular section at the centre of the black monochrome inner surface.[71]. Furumark included the Ialysos bowl in his LH IIIC : 1 late, Granary Style (FM 50, 14). A rather similar pattern is found on an amphoriskos from Ialysos[72]. The grave is one of Furumark's "type-graves" for his phase LH IIIC : 1b[73]. It may well be significant for the chronology that the reserved space inside at the bottom is evidently not found on monochrome deep bowls until phase 2 in Lefkandi[74]. Another parallel to the pattern is found on a deep bowl from Acrocorinth[75]. A deep bowl with antithetic spirals surrounding a central triglyph, similar to the one in question, was evidently found in Tarsus[76]. The bowl from Ialysos grave 17 was analysed by R. E. Jones and C. Mee, and was shown to be manufactured of local clay[77]. I suggest that 1,11, together with 1,12 and 1,13, as outlined infra, should be placed in a middle/late phase of LH IIIC.

1,12. The overall shape of the jar is similar to the developed types of "octopus jars"[78]. The change in this type of stirrup jar from early IIIC to middle IIIC is excellently illustrated through the development of 1,2 to 1,12/13. The same development can be seen from the stirrup jar *Ialysos* NT 83 : 4[79] to *Ialysos* NT 72 : 2B (12714)[80]. The first shows the same two stemmed spirals around the spout as 1,12, while the second has a closely related pattern of antithetic spirals in the handle zone. Thus I at least partly agree with A. Furumark, who placed NT 83 in his LH IIIC : 1a,, while NT 72 was placed in IIIC : 1b[81]. I should, however, emphasize that the grave NT 72 does not seem to me as homogeneous as proposed by A. Furumark. The piriform stirrup jar is undoubtedly IIIA 2[82], and the "rosette bowl" (12720) can hardly be later than "early IIIC". Thus the grave was evidently used for at least three burials (even if only one skeleton was recovered). Another, rather close parallel could be cited from Kalymnos[83].

1,13. This stirrup jar is evidently of the same type as that above, but much smaller. The same motif is seen on a stirrup jar from Pilona[84] and on one from Perati[85].

Passia Grave 1 – Summary of Dating

Thus grave 1 was in use in the LH IIIA 2 (/early B) period and in the early- middle/late IIIC phase. Grave no. 1 should therefore be considered a type example of the habit of re-using tombs in the LH IIIC period, a habit not least common in the Dodecanese[86]. In grave 1 some of the earlier pottery was evidently removed from the chamber, while other pieces were left inside and lay together with the early IIIC pottery. Contrary to circumstances on the Mainland, earlier grave goods are generally supposed to have been cleared out of graves in the Dodecanese[87]. Grave 1 thus seems to reflect a mixture of the two types of custom.

Grave 2

2,1. The shape is quite like that of 1,6, but the piece is somewhat higher. However, the low type with simple bands on the belly without thinner lines probably indicates a dating early in LH IIIC. The depressed shape is rather similar to that of two stirrup jars in the National Museum, Copenhagen[88]. The first a FS 171, the other probably a FS 176[89]. The pattern is found in handle zones on stirrup jars from LH IIIA 2[90]. The classification is rather unsafe, but the syntactical composition of the decoration might well be indicative.

2,2. As in the case of 2,1, the dating of this type is evidently dubious. The group FS 249 seems to be rather inhomogeneous and Furumark's dating (LH IIIA 2- C 1) depends mainly on typological criteria and too few contexts.

The semiglobular, deep type with a vertical handle standing almost at a right angle to the spout seems to be comparatively rare. One example from Apollakia, Rhodes[91], was dated by Furumark to LH IIIA 2. A rather similar bowl from Pilona was dated by Mee to LH IIIB[92]. Another parallel comes from Tanagra grave 115. This seems to contain vases from the LH II period and LH IIIB – the last being the spouted bowl[93]. Prosymna grave 51,805[94] also contained parallels. Several closely related pieces were found in graves at the cemeteries of Eleona and Langada on Kos : Eleona grave 15[95], Eleona grave 20[96], Langada grave 23[97], Langada grave 59[98]. Several fragments of spouted bowls, found in the settlement material from Seraglio, Kos, were classified by Morricone among the IIIC types, FS 298[99]. The pattern should probably be compared with decoration on skyphoi of the late IIIB and early IIIC[100]. Mainly considering the evidence from Kos and the pattern, I reckon a dating of the bowl 2,2 within the limits late IIIB/ early IIIC to be quite safe.

2,3. The type should be safely classified as FS 176[101]. The flower pattern with joining semi-circles is not very common. A rather similar one was seen at Asine[102]. Another example is found on the somewhat later octopus stirrup jar from Langada T. 39[103]. A dating early in LH IIIC seems reasonable.

2,4. The brazier FS 316 was rather carefully dealt with by C. Mee[104]. It seems safely attested in all periods from IIIA 2 to IIIC.

2,5. The short sword should be reckoned among Sandar's type F swords, or more accurately Catling's type Fii[105]. The characteristic features are the narrow pommel, the deep flanges, the square shoulders and rather narrow, flat blade. Furthermore, the pommel is wider than the handguard. There are no rivet holes in the blade of 2,5. The distribution pattern and typological characteristics have been discussed at length by the above authors. I shall only add references to a few pieces that have appeared later;
– Hexalophos, W. Thessaly (tumulus burial)[106].
– Surbo, Lecce in Apulia[107].

The dirk or dagger from the Asklepieion on Kos should probably be counted among Catling's type Fi[108]. Thus the sword 2,5 is the only Fii type definitely found on Rhodes[109]. The chronology of the type is derived from a number of contexts. The pieces from the hoards in Mycenae were discussed by T. G. Spyropoulos[110], who proposes a dating in the late 13th to 12th century. However, the hoards are difficult to associate precisely with the usual chronology for pottery. Two important graves on Kos contained Fii swords – Langada T. 46 with one burial contained a sword very like ours, date LH IIIB late[111]. Likewise close to our piece is the sword from Langada T. 53, a grave probably containing more than one burial. Except for one Zygouries kylix, the grave should evidently be dated within the early IIIC period – probably the sword should be too[112]. I should like to point out that the shoulders on the earlier sword from grave 46 are more rounded than those on the sword from grave 53. An important Fii sword from Perati grave 38 should be dated to a rather advanced stage of LH IIIC. This short sword perhaps represents a more advanced stage of development with parallel grooves in the middle of the tongue[113]. Hence it should be emphasized that all safely dated Fii swords point to a dating in the IIIC period. The only exception seems to be Langada T. 46 with shoulders more rounded than those of the rest of the group. For these reasons LH IIIC should likewise be the dating of Passia 2,5.

2,6. In Langada T. 10 were found two extremely close parallels said to be of lead or silver (the Copenhagen ring was not recognisable as silver until it was cleaned). L. Morricone describes the pieces as being "della tipica forma della tarda eta del bronzo...", but cites no parallels[114]. The grave furthermore contained the famous violin-bow fibula with two dots. The pottery is all LH IIIC[115].

2,7. The simple band-shaped finger-rings are evidently unusual in Mycenaean graves from the Dodecanese. They should be dated in accordance with the other items in the grave.

2,8.[116]. The small knife should be included in Sandars' class 1a without flanges to the haft. The classification is rather broad and Catling considers the class in general to occur throughout the Late Minoan and Late Helladic periods. The earlier specimens are listed by Sandars[117]. As class 1a is both very inhomogeneous and very large, I shall restrict myself to mentioning only closely related items from the Dodecanese. A specimen from *Ialysos* NT gr. 32 bears some resemblance to our knife[118]. The vast number of vases in this tomb should all be dated to the LH IIIC period[119]. Very close is the knife from Eleona T. 15[120] – the pottery is early IIIB and (mainly) IIIC. The above-mentioned Langada gr. 46 likewise contained a knife closely related to *2,8*[121]. The grave should be dated late LH IIIB. Thus the knife seems comfortably at home among the other items in tomb 2.

Passia Grave 2 – Summary of Dating

The burial in Passia grave 2 should thus be dated early in the LH IIIC period – even if a few elements might point towards late LH IIIB. The grave may have been partly plundered. If we consider the sherds found in the dromos as fragments of bowls from "previous" burials, thus representing a custom safely attested in grave 1, the sherds should either be of the same age as burials in the grave or indicate a *terminus post quem* for the items found in the grave. The most interesting and illuminating piece is undoubtedly sherd a on Fig. 20. A more or less deep band and pattern composed of concentric isolated semicircles (FM 43) is a common feature on deep bowls from several places in the Aegean, even if variations in detail are considerable. On Crete it should thus be considered a standard LM IIIB-C type found mainly in the Knossos Area[122]. A LM IIIB deep bowl exported to Cyprus was found in Hala Sultan Tekke, tomb 2[123]. More or less close parallels are also found on the Mainland : Asine, Levandis sector[124], Tiryns on a deep bowl painted inside[125] and Kalapodi, likewise from early LH IIIC[126]. A somewhat diverging variant in panel was found on a deep bowl in a LH IIIB 1 context at Mycenae[127]. Thus the sherd should not be dated prior to the late LH IIIB phase, which confirms a dating of grave 2 in LH IIIC. Sherd b on Fig. 20 probably derives from a kylix. The quirk pattern (FM 48) is very common and difficult to date more precisely – as pointed out infra[128]; painted kylikes are found on Rhodes even in the late LH IIIB phase.

Grave 4

No chronological implications could be drawn from the distribution of artifacts in the grave.

4,1. The majority of jars classified FS 35 by Furumark was found on Rhodes. The group is rather inhomogeneous and the borderline between it and the genuine piriform jars is rather vague. Furumark considers a Copenhagen jar, from Apollakia, rather close to *4,1*[129], to be IIIB. The jar 4,1 should be dated in the late LH IIIB period from its grave 4 context.

4,2. This jug is probably one of the most astonishing finds from the Passia graves. It was depicted by Vermeule and Karageorghis, who placed it in "the late period" (late 13th to early 12th cent.), indicating that it "may come from an unknown site in Asia Minor"[130]. It must be admitted that the pictorial style is quite unusual for Southern Rhodes where, for instance, the octopus stirrup jars are never found.
The shape FS 120/121 is, among other things, characterized by the handle starting below the rim. The borderline between the two classes is evidently rather ambiguous but *4,2* is obviously most closely related to the main part of FS 120 mentioned by Furumark. The flat or very low base contrasted with the lowfoot seems to be quite a significant typological criterion for distinguishing between LH IIIB and C (although not totally unambiguous, however). In the Dodecanese close parallels respecting shape and decorative syntax are found at *Ialysos* OT 35[131], Ialysos NT 38 : 1[132], and – according to Furumark – Ialysos NT 59, 4–5. The chronological pattern of all three graves is rather confusing – in NT 59, however, nothing seems to be later than IIIB. The shape is known from several sites on the Mainland : from chamber tomb 527 at Mycenae, in a context ranging from IIIA to

IIIC[133], and a far closer parallel from Zygouries in a pure LH IIIB – perhaps even late IIIB – context[134]. None was found in the Prophitis Elias cemetery at Tiryns. The chamber tomb cemetery of Deiras in Argos contained quite a few jugs recalling *4,2*. This group was dated Late IIIA 2 or IIIB by Deshayes[135]. More precisely, we have DV 28 from T. XIV in IIIB, DV 109 from T. XXVIII bis in LH IIIA 2, and DV 156 and DV 154 in IIIB. The closest parallel is from grave XIV. In settlement material from Mycenae, FS 121 occurs throughout longer periods – thus also in LH IIIB 2 contexts[136]. Several other parallels could be cited – nothing contradicts a dating in the LH IIIB period.

As pointed out by Vermeule and Karageorghis, the bird is drawn rather specially and it is actually difficult to compare with other Aegean styles. The iconography seems – to me – essentially to show some relations with the Cypriote "Rude Style", Vermeule and Karageorghis' "Pastoral Style". Among closer parallels is a specific Enkomi group, called Group (C) by D. Anson[137]. Pieces of this group seem to be considered "Middle Pastoral" by Vermeule and Karageorghis[138]; Anson points to a dating in early LC III[139]. A rather close parallel to the design, characterized by having "isolated semicircles" in the body of the bud, was found at Mycenae[140]. The sherd originates from an A-type skyphos with black interior. The dating is LH IIIC. Even if quite a few related patterns could be cited, with respect to style and to details in the pattern, the jug should be considered a local, late LH IIIB product; its decoration being probably a local forerunner of the later LH IIIC bud decoration[141]. An indication of the existence of a local Dodecanesian tradition for similar patterns is given in the unique settlement material from Seraglio, Kos[142]. Perhaps this indicates that at least some of the Kos material should be dated in late IIIB rather than in IIIC. A late IIIB krater from Koukounaries is probably of a related style[143].

4,3. As elsewhere in the Mycenaean World, the deep bowl is a type rare in graves. For Tiryns, Chr. Podzuweit divided the A-skyphos into six types. According to this division, our piece should be counted among Podzuweit's type 3 : "– mit einem ausgesparten Innen- – und breiten Aussenband", an innovation in the LH IIIB 2 phase[144]. The broad band on the outside of the rim of skyphoi that must still be classified as A-types is not usual in the Argolid, but at Tiryns it is sometimes found in IIIB 2 contexts[145] and in

IIIC on skyphoi with black paint inside[146]. All should be dated in the early IIIC phase. The deep bowls of the Argolid are usually higher and have a more curved section than that of the Rhodian piece. The type of rather deep band is also found on Crete, where neither antithetic spirals nor panelled style occur before the transitional phase to IIIC[147]. Antithetic spirals similar to those on *4,3* around a panel are found quite abundantly in IIIB 2 Tiryns[148], but not at Mycenae[149]. In Lefkandi the pattern was found in a LH IIIB context[150] and in Koukounaries on Paros in IIIB 2/early C[151]. Rather related patterns and quite substantial rim bands are first and foremost common in Cyprus. According to F. Schachermeyr, "die klassische Spiralantithese mit Triglyphe" was primarily found in "late LH IIIB" in the period of the "Ashlar Towns"[152]. Fairly good parallels could be cited from Enkomi IIIA[153]. Skyphoi with antithetic spirals of the stemmed type were found in the important Kition T. 9, upper burial, dated to late IIIB by V. Karageorghis[154].

I propose that the deep bowl no. *4,3*, like the jug *4,2*, should be considered a representative of the late IIIB period in Rhodes.

4,4. The shape is evidently a common LH IIIB/ early C type, but the pattern is unique. In the Argolid the production of patterned kylikes probably ceased already towards the end of the IIIB 1 period[155], but, as suggested by C. Mee, patterned kylikes continued in use at Ialysos throughout IIIB[156]. I agree with Mee on this point and consider the kylix no. *4,4*, with its very specific variation of the antithetic spiral pattern, to be a representative of the later LH IIIB patterned kylikes. A somewhat related pattern is found on a kylix from Kastanás in Macedonia in a LH IIIB context[157].

4,5. Compared to the majority of amphorae classed by Furumark in his group FS 36/37, this amphora differs in several aspects. The cylindrical neck is relatively long in relation to the body and the handles are placed unusually low, terminating downwards just above the largest width of the jar. The decorated panel covers the entire upper part of the ovoid body. A few, somewhat related jars are found on the Mainland, e.g. Mycenae[158]. However, this piece may rather have some affinity with specimens from Cyprus, where the typological details emphasized supra are both common and closely related – the tendency to extend the decorated panel might likewise reflect the influence of Cypriot kraters[159]. These common Levanto-Mycenaean types of jar were treated by V. Karageorghis and dated within the LH IIIB period , based on an Aegean IIIA prototype[160]. In contrast, the space-filling panelled patterns are very unlike the Cypriot style and, for that matter, even without parallel in the Aegean as well. Here, however, the panelled style is naturally rather common, not least in the IIIB 2 period. While the syntax of the pattern is extremely unique, the single elements are not rare in the Mycenaean decorative repertoire. A few comments should be added on the vertical "joining U-pattern" which, especially in the antithetic composition, seems somewhat unusual. In the Dodecanese the pattern is found on a LH IIIB kylix from Kalymnos, otherwise it seems more usual in the Eastern Mediterranean, where examples are found in Cyprus and Ras Shamra/Ugarit[161]. These Eastern parallels point in general towards a dating in LH IIIB, but not particularly late. A single row of vertical "joining U-patterns" is found in "frühes IIIC" at Tiryns[162], and a double antithetic row on a IIIC skyphos from the Athenian Acropolis[163]. Running quirks on the rim of three-handled jars are very common, but the hanging, double arches around the neck of the collar are extraordinary[164].

4,6. The ovoid two-handled amphora with the rather short neck might perhaps be considered a type of domestic jar. No close parallels can be cited.

4,7. The shape FS 182 has a wide, if not entirely uniform distribution within the Aegean as well as in the Eastern Mediterranean. In the Dodecanese the shape is rather common in the Langada cemetery on Kos[165], at Ialysos, according to C. Mee, the shape occurs in at least four graves, with quite a few in OTA[166]. In Southern Rhodes the shape is quite usual[167]. C. Mee suggested in his dissertation from 1975 that FS 182 was a locally made type and should be dated late in LH IIIB (IIIB 2). Later, he evidently came to prefer a more general dating withing the LH IIIB phase considering the type to be imported from the Argolid[168]. One suspects that he changed his opinion as a result of his original idea that contact with the Argolid was intense during the LH IIIB 1 period, but decreased drastically during LH IIIB 2. Because the specimen from Tomb A[169] proved to be an import from the Argolid[170], a IIIB 2 dating became questionable. As pointed out below, however, I at least consider FS 182 with band-shaped quirk such as 4,7 to be a late IIIB product. Perhaps the assumed lack of relations between

the IIIB 2 Mainland and the Dodecanese is partly a question of different sources of material, local traditions and insufficient recognition of the chronological structure of graves (see infra p..). It should be noted that Wulf Rudolf considered the type to be late LH IIIB 2 in the Profitis Elias cemetery at Tiryns[171].

In order to obtain a safer dating of the stirrup jar, I would like to study in greater detail the chronology of the highly characteristic pattern of the band-shaped "circumcurrent quirk". The "band-shaped quirk" itself probably does not occur until LH IIIB 1, when it appears from the very beginning on stems of kylikes from the "Potter's shop" in Zygouries[172]. A related kylix was found at Ras Shamra/Ugarit[173]. The same kind of vertical pattern in a panel is found on a LH IIIB 2 deep bowl from Mycenae[174]. Turning to Tiryns, several examples of the band-shaped "circumcurrent quirk" can be cited. From the so-called Epichosis, the pattern occurs on a stirrup jar (FS 173)[175] and on A-skyphoi[176]; on skyphoi from early LH IIIC Tiryns Unterburg[177]; and a vertical pattern from a krater of the same period (?)[178]. A very nice example of the pattern on a LH IIIB 2 bowl, Tiryns Unterburg, was excavated by Klaus Kilian in 1981[179]. In Mycenae the band-shaped "circumcurrent quirk" appears in combination with N-patterns on a FS 173 stirrup jar from the West House[180]. This "destruction" context should be considered the latest in LH IIIB 1 from Mycenae[181]. In LH IIIB 2 deposits at Mycenae the pattern occurs on deep bowls[182]. Strangely enough, the shape FS 182 is not found among settlement material from Mycenae, nor from the chamber tombs.

To conclude : the pattern of the band-shaped "circumcurrent quirk" occurs in the Argolid from the latest phase of the LH IIIB 1 period, continues through the LH IIIB 2 phase, and still exists in the early LH IIIC period. In these late Tiryns contexts the pattern has a more sharp look than the earlier examples have. Hence, we should probably conclude that the stirrup jar 4,7 should be placed rather late in the LH IIIB period – the time that we term IIIB late. The stirrup jars FS 182 are hardly exported from the Argolid.

At Ialysos the pattern was found on a FS 182 stirrup jar from OTA[183] and on FS 176 stirrup jars from NT 83 and 84[184]. NT 83 is one of Furumark's archetypal graves for IIIC : 1a[185]. NT 84 with the imported LM IIIB octopus stirrup jar is at any rate a IIIC grave – but not entirely IIIC : 1a in the Furumark sense[186]. The stirrup jar by far the closest to ours is the well-known one from Ras Shamra grave 37[187]. The FS 182 shape is rather common in the tombs of Ras Shamra/Ugarit and Minet-el-Beidha. The other decorative elements cannot give more exact information relating to the chronology, but none contradicts a dating in the late IIIB period.

4,8. Shape FS 9 has an extremely wide distribution and is very common from the Greek Mainland, the Islands and the Levant. Not least in Cyprus is this type of krater common. It should be emphasized that it often proves very difficult to distinguish between shapes FS 7–9. What is of interest in this connection is that shapes rather similar to *4,8* are found in good late IIIB (IIIB 2) contexts; for instance, in the Tiryns Epichosis[188] and from the LH IIIB 2/early C settlement of Koukounaries on Paros[189]. In the Argolid virtually no kraters have been found in graves, but they constitute quite a characteristic element in recently excavated settlement material from Mycenae and Tiryns. In the Dodecanese the situation seems rather similar if not so pronounced. No kraters were found in the Eleona and Langada cemeteries on Kos; however, in the "Seraglio" settlement material the krater (including FS 9) is a common shape[190]. With respect to FS 7–9, C. Mee mentions five pieces from Ialysos[191]. Kraters from Southern Rhodes are represented by two from Vati and one from Apollakia that are now in the National Museum, Copenhagen[192], while one was found in the grave from Pilona[193]. Quite a few sherds from kraters were found in the small, fortuitous surface collections from the Apollakia area and from the cemetery of Apsaktiras (also dating from IIIC)[194].
The decoration is extraordinary and undoubtedly points to local manufacture. The lower part of the central hybrid flower pattern on the front is a rather common IIIB pattern closely related to that of the Vati krater in Copenhagen[195]; the cross-hatched oval figures at the top are more specific though. A related pattern is found on a IIIB 1 kylix from the "Potter's shop" at Zygouries[196], while another is seen on a large krater from Ras Shamra/Ugarit[197]. The stemmed spiral to the left of the central flower pattern probably points towards a late IIIB or later dating, while the strange "bird" to the right seems most like a botched attempt. The remaining decorative elements are traditional in the Mycenaean IIIB/C repertoire, but parallels for the construction of the patterns are difficult to find. The lozenge pattern looks rather IIIC like, using Furumark's chronology; it points, however, also towards the

style of the bird-vase *4,2*. An almost identical motif is seen on a deep bowl from Tiryns Unterburg found in a IIIB 2 context[198]. The various flower motifs are not usual; in style they recall motifs from Cypriot kraters[199], but the central row of decoration connected with this pattern might be specifically Rhodian/Dodecanesian. A dating in late IIIB seems not unreasonable after all.

4,8 a-d. See supra under *1,9.*

4,9. The shape of the bell krater was treated in some detail in connection with the krater *1,4* (supra). Furumark considered shape FS 281 to be a IIIB type, while a related motif on the body zone of a miniature hydria NT 20 : 11 from Ialysos was dated in the LH IIIC period[200]. In contrast to the Ialysos specimen, however, this pattern shows an astonishing similarity to U-shaped anthers of the IIIA 2 period[201]. One further bell krater of FS 281 shape was found on Rhodes – Ialysos NT 53 : 3. C. Mee considered this a IIIB import from Boeotia[202]. It has a more rounded, closed shape than our krater, which is undoubtedly "homemade". As pointed out supra (*4,8*), the reason why so few kraters (both FS 9 and FS 281/82) are found on Rhodes is that this shape was not normally included in the grave goods.

4,10. The depressed globular stirrup jar with a rather flat top (FS 173) is a common shape in LH IIIB 1 Mycenae and is even found in LH IIIB 2[203]. The U-shaped anther in the centre of the flower motif is similar to that on the bell krater *4,9*. The type of flower pattern FM 18, 82–83 was evidently used in the LH IIIA 2 phase in Mycenae[204], but was not found in IIIB contexts in Mycenae[205]. Furumark's statement on this point has thus been confirmed by actual excavations. This pattern should therefore (at least from an Argivocentric point of view) be considered a characteristic Rhodian IIIA 2 survival in the IIIB period – a phenomenon which might be most significant in Southern Rhodes[206].

4,11. The large piriform ovoid jar probably most resembles Furumark's FS 37 but, as the piece is undoubtedly a local domestic type, it is hard to find relevant parallels. A jar just as badly reconstructed, from Seraglio, Kos, seems close[207]. The very open spiral is extremely common – closest to FM 46,54, and found from "LH IIIA 2 – C : 1e". Nevertheless the shape indicates a date rather in the later part of this time span.

4,12.[208].

The low conical cup *4,12* is of the FS 250 type dated by Furumark within the probable time span LH IIIB-IIIC : 1e. As pointed out supra (p. 99), the deep type of semiglobular spouted cup was quite common in the Eleona and Langada cemeteries. In Langada, however, even a shallow type rather similar to our piece was found in T 46[209]. This grave should be considered late IIIB or at least mainly late IIIB[210].

4,13. There is some uncertainty regarding important details of the appearance of this jug. It is undoubtedly globular and only slightly depressed but the extent of the actual restoration is not mentioned ("was there a spout ?"). Thus it is extremely uncertain if the jug really did have a trefoil lip as indicated on the drawing. Trefoil lips are almost nonexistent in Mycenaean pottery[211]. Furthermore it looks as if the round handle extends at a right angle to the spout – but this is somewhat difficult to establish with any certainty. The jug is probably local, but the type is evidently not usual in graves. In Eleona and Langada this type of "bucchero" ware was found in several graves. A jug rather resembling our specimen was found in one of the latest IIIC graves in the Langada cemetery, T 50[212].

4,14. Like the figurine Apsaktiras no. 5[213], this one should be classified among Lisa French's relatively rare "High-waisted Psi type"[214]. These two would appear to be the first to be published from the Dodecanese where figurines are not common in tombs until LH IIIC[215]. As the type is found both on the Mainland and in the Eastern Mediterranean[216], it is hardly surprising to find it on Rhodes. The type should be dated between LH IIIA 2 and IIIB, where examples were found "even in the latest phase"[217]. As far as can be judged from present evidence, the type does not cross over into LH IIIC, where terracotta idols change both in shape and decoration.

4,15. The oblong, flat beads, "Curls of Hair", were studied carefully by N. Yalouries[218]. As emphasized by this author, such "curls of hair" were used for diadems, which is in good accordance with Kinch's information that they were found "close to one of the skulls". The pendants *4,15,1* are closely related to the thirty-four curls from the Kladeos Cemetery, north of Olympia, and to some Ialysos pieces in the British Museum, depicted by Yalouries[219]. Yalouries considered them to "belong to an earlier stage in the evolution of the curl motif" – earlier than exam-

ples from two graves near Olympia dated within the time range IIIB-C[220]. In Ialysos the type was found in NT 28, NT 31 and NT 53 – the first is a IIIA 2 grave, the second a IIIA 2 grave including a few IIIA 1 pots, while the third is a purely LH IIIB grave (having both early and late IIIB characteristics). Evidently the type does not occur in LH IIIC graves – except probably in Achaea[221]. Beads like *4,15,6* were found at Ialysos NT XX[222], dated by Mee in LH IIIC, and in the somewhat earlier grave Langada T 38 in Coo[223]. Beads such as these are common in Mycenaean graves[224]. I have not found good counterparts for the remaining beads.

Passia Grave 4 – Summary

The majority of the pottery from Passia grave 4 seems therefore to be locally produced. However, some ornamental and even some morphological elements seem to point towards Cyprus, in one case perhaps towards Crete (4,3). The pattern on the kylix 4,4 has an interesting parallel from far distant Kastanás in Macedonia. It is a characteristic feature that no strictly Argivian connections can be traced. Neither the distribution pattern of the grave goods nor the stratigraphical observations gave rise to chronological groupings. In the above analysis I have argued that the whole group might be dated within one single phase which, as a preliminary proposal, I term late LH IIIB. It should be emphasized, though, that some of the vase types evidently had quite a long lifetime; furthermore, several traits could not be inserted more precisely than within a late IIIB/early IIIC frame. Hence there is a possibility that this group of pottery is not entirely pre-IIIC in the Argivian sense of the term, rather perhaps late IIIB/transitional IIIB-C/early IIIC (?) and contemporary with the phase defined in the Cyclades[225].

Various finds from Apsaktiras, Vati

Pottery

1. The antithetic spiral pattern and the wavy line in the triglyph are related to the pattern on the deep bowl Passia no. *4.3;* the bowl, however, is much smaller and shallower and has no broad band on the lip. Shape and decoration indicate a dating in LHIII B as a very general statement. I propose a dating in the middle part – when comparing with Argive dating[226]. There is, however, a rather astonishing parallel from the socalled box gamma 67 material in the Heraklion

Museum[227] – although the Cretan skyphos is monochrome painted on the inside. The dimensions of the Apsaktiras skyphos likewise point towards Crete. This even gives possibilities of a Late B date.

2–4. The three vases, said to be from "grave 21", were published in *CVA* DK and treated by Furumark and/or Mee :
– no. 2 was dated by Furumark ("probably") in his LHIII C : 1 phase (FS 194, 17), while Mee prefered "uncertain"[228].
– no. 3 was dated by Mee in LHIII B (FS 192) and
– no. 4 was placed by Furumark in LHIII C : 1c (FS 176 : 38) and by Mee in LHIII C 1[229].

5. The psi-idol is very closely related to the figurine from Passia grave 4[230].

6–8. The undecorated kylikes are difficult to date more precisely. The shallow bowl is of Furumark's very general type 204, the plain handle cup that shows considerable variation. Its occurrence in LHIII C seems confirmed by the bowls from Asine, Chamber tomb 1[231].

Bronzes

9. The knife should be included among Sandars' Type 1a[232], but the S-curved profile of the blade is unusual. In general Sandars' very simple distinction between knives without flanges (1a) and with flanges (1b) gives no important references to the chronological or distributional aspects of the knives. Beside the S-curved profile, the very short handle is probably of significance. The proportion between handle and blade is around 3.8 (index). The short handle-zone must indicate that the piece was probably not used as an "ordinary" knife. The S-curved outline is found on a knife with light flanges (1b) from the Dictaean Cave[233], but otherwise the similarity is not striking. Milojcic considered the curving of the blades to show Central European affinities[234].

10. Is a usual specimen of Sandars' type 1a. It deviates from the majority of knives in the group by having a rather curved back and a blade thickened near the handle. A Cretan knife has a somewhat similar outline[235]. Milojcic evidently suggests a rather late date (1250–950 BC) for this piece. Another similar piece was found in the interesting tholos tomb close to Agh. Theklas on Tinos – it seems quite well dated in LHIII B[236]. A III B dating is probably preferable for our piece.

11. The knife is in Sandars' type 1b group. As in the case of no. 9, it should be noted that the blade/handle-zone index is high : 3.37. Ialysos NT 59 seems a close parallel[237]. According to Mee, this grave contained pottery of LHIII A2-B date, but mainly III B[238]. The knife Ialysos NT 26 shows some similarity[239]. The grave was dated LHIII A2 by Mee[240].

12. The knife can be included in N. K. Sandars' "Siana group" of bronzes[241], and is especially close to the knife from Siana itself. Sandars considered this group of bronzes to be inspired by Levantine prototypes and to be dated in the 12th century (cit.). As pointed out by Mee, the pottery from Ialysos OT : 27 is undoubtedly III A2/B and not III B/C as presumed by Sandars[242]. Its distribution is restricted to the eastern Aegean with examples from Ialysos, Colophon, Fraktin and Troy[243]. Moreover a specimen from Armenochori in Astypalia can now be added[244]. This piece has a special relationship with Ialysos OT 27 and Colophon. The grave context gives no new information regarding chronology.[245] Even if the knives in the group are morphologically related, they differ rather markedly in technical respects. Thus the Armenochori, Ialysos OT 27, and Colophon pieces have flanges of bronze sheet, like the F2 sword from Passia grave 2,5, while the Siana and Apsaktiras knives were probably entirely cast in a two-piece mould. As pointed out, nothing really seems to indicate a dating within the III C period. If Sandars' very reasonable idea of a Levantine origin for the type is to be retained, we must consider the possibility that these bronzes are rather the results of the earlier-mentioned[246] late III B relationship than of raids by the Sea People. The evidence from Ras Shamra too is a better fit to this assumption.

Various beads, etc.

Beads nos. 1–9 are all of the usual LHIII types, also found in Passia grave 4 and at Kattavia[247]. The small granulated gold bead is a simple variant of a type found, e.g. in the Tiryns hoard[248]. With respect to the beads of stone and clay, the double-cone pieces may be spindle whorls, while the others could be buttons or beads[249].

Comments on the survey material from Apsaktiras

Most of the sherd material from Apsaktiras was recovered from the southern plateau. A great number of sherds lay on the surface and only a few of the more significant pieces were collected. Besides some Turkish sherds, only Mycenaean material was recovered. Hence it is hardly necessary to emphasize the fortuitous character of this material. The following is an attempt at a brief chronological evaluation of the more significant sherds (the references do not intend to be exhaustive).

Among sherds found "Near grave 11", no. 1 with the rather characteristic rhomboid chequer pattern may be from a krater. The pattern seems unusual. A similar pattern is found on a rather famous amphoroid, pictorial krater from Enkomi[250], which should be dated within the LHIII A2 period. Other parallels are found on kraters as far away as Scoglio del Tonno in Apulia[251]. Biancofiore underlines the relations with Cypriote fabrics. A dating in LHIII A2 seems reasonable. The more usual pattern on no. 3, likewise probably from a krater, could be paralleled with III B1 settlement material from Mycenae[252]. Finally the fragment of the stirrup jar no. 4 with its multiple-stem pattern well fits a LHIII A2/B1 date. The straight-sided, conical bowl no. 5 and the pithos rim no. 6 may be local types. The jug from grave 13 must likewise be considered local and is not easily datable. It should, however, be emphasized that trefoil-lipped jugs are rather late in the Mycenaean pottery repertoire.

The monochrome krater from the "Cutting in rock" no. 1 is of rather closed shape, the thickening on the rim being unusual as krater rims normally seem to turn outwards at a sharp angle. The type might be local. The closed-shape jar no. 2 with the large spiral in combination with a scale pattern might perhaps be III A1 in date, but could also be from the shoulder zone of a tall III A2 jar (which is more likely). The diaper net on no. 3 hardly occurs before LHIII A1, but could, of course, be later.

Among the sherds collected from various finding places, the flat plate or dish no. 1 must be a local type – the shape might be related to that seen on *CVA* DK, Pl. 55, 4–5. The pattern on sherd no. 2 has an exact counterpart in the decoration of the shoulder zone of a large piriform jar in Copenhagen[253]. Sherd no. 2 must likewise be from the shoulder zone of a large three-handled piriform jar and should be dated in III B (the shape is closer to Passia 4,1 than to the Granto jar). Finally, sherd no. 3 from a closed-shape jar (perhaps a squat jar with angular profile (FS 94) ?) having parallel chevrons, stemmed spiral and panel must be LHIII B in date – but parallels prove difficult to find.

The most interesting group of material is that labelled "Concentration of sherds in the Mycenaean necropolis". Of these, sherd no. 1 has a section that is common for a krater with splaying rim. The pattern differs from the canonical variant by curving upwards, not hanging. On the Mainland there are several cases of the isolated semicircle motif on kraters[254]. These patterns are all built up of reversed loops in panels. On deep bowls the pattern occurs already from III B (for instance in the Tiryns Epichosis). S. Hood published a krater from Emporio on Chios, which is of greater similarity ot our specimen. Hood dated it in phase Myc III C : 1d[255]. The most convincing parallel however derives from an unpublished krater from the Tiryns epichosis, which indicates a safe dating in the later part of the LH IIIB phase[256]. The krater no. 2 is hard to class more precisely, while the cup no. 3 might be classified in general as a shallow semiglobular cup with horizontal handle[257]. The large open bowl with thickening on the inside is rather peculiar and probably a local speciality.

All four sherds on Fig. 73 (nos. 7–7a) are from the same jar (or perhaps two different ones). They probably come from the handle zone of a three-handled biconical jar of the type *CVA* DK, Pl. 42 : 5 said to be from Asklipio[258]. The pattern on the four sherds (7–7a) shows at least seven inscribed triangles. On the Asklipio jar the number of triangles varies from five to seven. In Rhodes Furumark evidently considered such a composition of triangles to be characteristic of the early III C : 1 period[259]. In the Argolid however it now seems to be attested that the pattern on the upper part of closed shape jars is not found until LH IIIC Fortgeschritten – Spät[260]. Thus these sherds are probably later than the above-mentioned characteristic Rhodian angular/techtonic style[261]. The remaining sherds from the concentration are small and difficult to date. No. 9 with motif related to FM 75,29 must be part of a panelled pattern of LH IIIC (late ?) date. The zone with vertical parallel lines is found in "Seraglio", Kos[262], all should be dated in the LH IIIC phase. A IIIC dating is also proposed for nos. 8–8a with the debased tassel motif[263]. Nothing probably contradicts the possibility of a IIIC dating for the rest of the sherds depicted on Figs. 73–74.

Apsaktiras, Vati – summary

Quite a few of the Rhodian Mycenaean vases kept in the National Museum, Copenhagen[264] have the provenance Apsaktiras. According to Arne Furumark and C. Mee they cover the time span from LH IIIA2 to LH IIIC1[265]. The typological and stylistic variations evidently embody quite a few local elements. As no local stratigraphical evidence is at hand, we have to rely on this traditional chronological perception, which will undoubtedly be altered as a result of future excavations[266].

Perhaps it might be suggested that the FS 182 stirrup jars[267] be placed in the late IIIB phase, contemporary with Passia grave 4. As pointed out supra[268], the stirrup jar CVA DK, Pl. 59,3 may be early IIIC in dating rather than IIIB as suggested by Mee. As to the IIIC pottery, perhaps at least the askos CVA DK, Pl. 46,7 and the jug CVA DK, Pl. 44,1, should be dated early in IIIC. The former piece has chevrons as do the jugs CVA DK, Pl. 44, 4–5[269], the latter has white paint on octopus arms[270]. The majority of the pottery dated to LH IIIC by Furumark and Mee may in fact prove to be rather early in the period.

The fortuitous surface collection of sherds confirms the dating of the cemetery within the time span LH IIIA2-C. While the sherds collected near the graves may mainly be derived from grave types of pottery, those from the SW area, "concentration of sherds in Mycenaean Necropolis", could well represent local settlement material from the LH IIIC period. Sherd no. 1 from this concentration derives from a LH IIIB (probably late) krater while the sherds 7–7a determine a dating later than that of the majority of pots found in the graves contemporary with IIIC-Fortgeschritten-spät/Lefkandi 2b and the Granary context in Mycenae. During their survey of the area R. Hope Simpson and J. F. Lazenby pointed out that there might have been a settlement as well as a cemetery on the rock – however no foundations were identified[271].

Kalovriou Vati

Apart from a general dating in LHIII, no more precise dating could be given to the graves from Kalovriou. The deep bowl CVA DK 2, Pl. 53, 8 is evidently a III A2 type.

Trapezies Paraelis, Apollakia

Comments on the survey material

The survey material gives an idea of the chronological distribution of use of the site.

Sherd no. 1 from grave 1 is from an open bowl.

The running spiral with the V-shaped figure[272] and the flower motif clearly point to a dating in LHIII A2. The very broad band on the lip is unusual for bowls of the period, and if the slightly curving small triangular sherd is to be interpreted as a bottom, then the shape of the bowl is unique in Mycenaean material. The section and the band on the rim indicate that no. 2 is from a III A2 kylix. The pattern to the left on Fig. 80 might be a multiple stem (FM 19) motif, while the pattern to the right is difficult to identify.

The sherds from graves 3, 6 and 7 on Fig. 81 are not easy to date precisely; the large sherd from grave 3 is probably from a large three-handle jar as that seen on Fig. 99, from Granto. Among the sherds from the dromos of grave 11, no. 1 (Fig. 82, middle row, left – note that it should be viewed upside down) comes from the upper part of a closed shape jar, a small thickening on the left of the sherd might have been part of a handle. The type of decoration is found on three-handled jars[273] and stirrup jars[274], a LHIII A2 dating seems safe. The same dating is suggested for the stirrup-jar handle zone no. 3. Sherd no. 1 from grave 14 should be classed among a rather rare type of kraters or bowls from the LH IIIA2 period, not from IIIC[275].

Both nos. 2 and 3 from grave 14 might well be dated in the III A2 period while no. 1 from grave 19, if classed as a large deep bowl, must be of rather late IIIC date. All sherds collected from grave 20 (Fig. 85) are probably of III A2 date. No. 1 is a quite unusual, evidently local piece. The various sherds depicted on Fig. 86 should likewise be dated in III A2, while no. 6 on Fig. 86 is a local piece difficult to date. A connection with tassel patterns would date the piece in LH IIIC.

Chimaro, Apollakia

The rim sherd no. 1 can hardly be more precisely dated. The pattern on no. 2 is perhaps too broad to be a whorl-shell pattern, but both designs could be parts of a pictorial design – perhaps a bird[276]. The sherd with zigzag pattern is undoubtedly part of a basket-handle belonging to a vase like that from Apollakia, now in Copenhagen[277]. Mee dates the Apollakia vase to LHIII C[278]. Because the reverse of this vase shows a somewhat detached version of pattern FM 62,26, I am inclined to agree with Mee's dating. The same dating should apply to the sherd with a spiral that is part of an antithetic spiral pattern.

Unpublished items having Apollakia as provenance

The unpainted cup no. 5525 is a very common type. A rather similar piece from Emporio, Chios, was dated by S. Hood to LHIII A, even if it was found in a III B grave[279]. The stirrup jar no. 5548 should be dated in the same phase. The one-edged "razor" no. 5601 should be classed with the very common Aegean "triangular" type of "razor" having only a slightly curved back[280]. Sandars considers the type to have developed late in (LM) LHIII A and to have been in use in III B and perhaps in III C. A few more closely related Dodecanesian pieces from Ialysos NT 4,21 and Langada T 25 should be cited. The first grave mainly contains LHIII A2 pottery and just a few III C pots, the Langada tomb likewise contains III A2 and III C pottery. I consider a dating of the "razors" to III A2 quite safe[281]. The lance or spearhead no. 5602 should be included in O. Höckmann's Group F, variant IV[282]. This group is characterized in particular by having straight blade edges and an angular transition between blade and socket. The group shows an Island Aegean distribution with a marked eastern Aegean distribution. The typological variation is, moreover, extraordinarily wide. A somewhat related piece was found at Ialysos close to grave NT VI[283]. The context affords no dating. Another (but somewhat longer) piece included in Höckmann's group G4 from Ialysos OT4 also shows some typological elements related to those of our piece. The tomb contains vases dated LHIII A/B[284]. The rather special facetted socket of no. 5602 is quite unusual. As this spearhead should, however, probably be dated in LHIII A2/B, Höckmann's statement that "Polygonaltülle" points rather towards the Protogeometric period may perhaps be considered not too general[285].

As the previous number, the spearhead inv.no. 5603 should be included in Höckmann's Group F, variant IV. Three rather related specimens were found on Kos[286]. The first was in the metal hoard found east of the Lapidario of the Asklepeion, dated LHII by Höckmann. The context, however, seems somewhat doubtful; furthermore the horned short sword of Sandars' class C1, which should probably give the dating, is rather atypical[287]. The two others originate from Eleona graves 6 or 7 containing, respectively, III C and A1 and III C pottery.

Apollakia – Summary

Among the 94 vases with provenance Apollakia, kept in the National Museum, Copenhagen, the majority evidently should be dated in the LH IIIA2 period, quite a number was, more or less safely, placed in the LH IIIB phase, while surprisingly few could safely be dated in the LH IIIC period[288]. As for the dating in general, reference should be made to the summary of the Apsaktiras graves and to the concluding chapters[289]. Among the LH IIIC pottery the amphoriskos, *CVA* DK, Pl. 43, 10, should probably be placed rather late in the development as suggested by Furumark, who fits it into his LH IIIC-1b phase.

The survey material from Trapezies Paraelis, the place from where our material in Copenhagen undoubtedly derives, confirms the impression of a dominance in the LH IIIA2 period. As in Apsaktiras, some of the items might well be considered domestic types of pottery.

From the vicinity of Kattavia

The pottery from the area called "Sto Granto" is not discussed in greater detail as all fits into the canonical III A2 scheme. The same dating is proposed for the grave from "Ta Tzingani". The kylikes on Kinch's sketch seem to be of the deep type with rather short stem. The knife of Sandars' type 1b should thus be dated in this phase too.

Other items having Kattavia as provenance

The Aegean fish hooks were treated in detail by H.-G. Buchholz, G. Jöhrens and I. Maull[290]. Four hooks are stated to be found in Ialysos, covering the time span LH IIIA2 to IIIC. The Kattavia piece (inv.no. 7701) should be dated in LH IIIA2, as the remaining items from this part of the island. There is no knowledge of how this piece was fixed to the line.
The beads are all common types in the Mycenaean World.

Various unpublished Rhodian Mycenaean objects found and bought by the Danish Expedition

Of this small group inv.no. 7566 is a rim sherd from a LHIII A2 kylix – the pattern with fringes is rather unusual, however. Inv.no. 12364 is an ordinary LHIII A2/B kylix. Of far greater interest are the two remaining stirrup jars. Jars of the same shape as inv.no. 12502 were examined in detail by A. Furumark and by E. Gjerstad[291]. Both agreed about the typological connection between a Cypriote jar from the Cesnola Collection[292] and the jar from Kerameikos grave S 106, illustrating the close relations between Cyprus and the Aegean. Gjerstad, however, dated the jars in his Proto-white painted/Submycenaean phase while Furumark argued a dating contemporary with his LHIII C : IC/LCyp III B(2) phase. Furumark noted that "the only difference between these vases (i.e. the Cypriote) and their Mycenaean counterparts is that the Cypriote specimens are comparatively tall"[293]. I should like to add that the Cypriote specimens are also slimmer and have the maximum width higher up the belly, while the "Mycenaean counterparts" are much closer to groups of traditional mainland late III C stirrup jars[294]. Therefore I rather doubt the chronological value of this comparison. Inv.no. 12502 is very obviously connected far more closely to the tall, slimmer Cypriote type "S". The Cypriote jar is not dated locally by context.

The decoration on our piece is characterized by its combination of old-fashioned motifs (scale pattern and zigzag, which are, however, not unusual throughout the LHIII C period), and strictly rectilinear patterns of later type. With respect to dating, the hour-glass-shaped pattern with cross-hatched rhomboid patterns (Fig. 115) is of great importance, as it can only be related to the Cypriote white-painted I/CGIA/PG repertoire[295] and not at all to the earlier LHIII C/LCIII B decorations. We must thus conclude that stirrup jar 12502 should be dated in a phase contemporary with the early Protogeometric, etc., in Cyprus; consequently also with the Submycenaean and/or transitional LHIII C/PG phase in Athens and other parts of the Greek Mainland, e.g., the Argolid[296].

As to the stirrup jar 12501, the decoration clearly points towards the Submycenaean period. Close parallels to the shape, however, are difficult to find. Submycenaean material is reported from the coast of Asia Minor, primarily from Miletus[297]. Furthermore an interesting piece from a grave in the neigbourhood of the village of Eski Hisar (ancient Stratonikeia) was published by J. C. Waldbaum and G. M. A. Hanfmann[298]. On this last jar vertical wavy lines are found in the same position as on our piece, but the shape is more globular. The pattern is found in a similar position on another globular stirrup jar from Langada T 50. The grave contained an amphoriskos related to SM types in Kerameikos[299]. More recently the pattern was found during the new excavations at Asine, where it was dated by Barbro Santillo Frizell in her final Mycenaean phase – contemporary with SM in Attica[300].

C. Summary of chronology and foreign relations

A note on Furumark's chronology

It is a common habit among scholars of Mycenaean archaeology to accept a setting up of the chronological framework based on successive styles or groups of styles of pottery. Even in very recent publications it is customary to classify pottery within a more or less agreed system. As chronological classification constitutes the basis for conclusions regarding cultural relations and settlement patterns, and often for far-reaching historical inferences, it is obvious that chronological matters must be treated with care. Moreover recent excavations in the Argolid and Euboea show that the chronology of Mycenaean pottery is more complicated than outlined in the traditional perception. Nevertheless, it is just as obvious that we still depend very heavily on this perception (with adjustments) when local stratigraphical material is not or only sparsely at hand – as is the situation in the Dodecanese. These circumstances may justify a brief comment on Furumark's chronology as his *MP* may still be considered the "bible" of the traditional thinking in this respect.

The fundamental concepts for Furumark's taxonomy and chronological evaluations are type and style. In an extensive footnote he rejects the "Swedish typology" (in Åberg's consistent version) in which an attempt was made to set up normative rules for the development of material culture by analogy with the evolution of organic life[301]. However, he accepts the typological method as such and "Theoretically, a qualified typological series is at the same time chronological". Even if "dating on purely typological grounds is a rather hazardous undertaking", "Mycenaean pottery is in possession of some qualities that make it permissible to a comparatively great extent to use the typological method for chronological purposes". As to the concept of style, Furumark throws caution to the winds, "The Mycenaean pottery is distinguished by a great uniformity of style : the general stylistic criteria apply to all contemporary vases, and, consequently, the separate classes of style form a chronological series".

With respect to the chronological aspects of the typological method, it has often been emphasized that even if quite a number (actually an infinite number) of recent and ancient empirical data are at hand, showing that qualified typological series illustrating chronological developments in the works of man could be established, it has never been possible to establish general laws (*a priori*) for such developments. Such laws are probably too specific to be of general acceptability. Thus for both prehistoric and historic material it is evident that the qualifications of such series must be provided through stratigraphical investigations. This was evidently acknowledged by Furumark : nevertheless he still thought that "qualified series" could be constructed for Mycenaean pottery.

The possibilities of confirming chronological evidence derived from typological and stylistic classification, through contextual and stratigraphic studies, were treated in detail by Furumark in his *Chronology*. However, as to the contextual analyses, the logical structure is basically hampered by the surprising statement that "The vases belonging to a certain find group may be arranged according to *Stylistic groups*"[302]. It follows from this statement that, when the closed find groups have "allowed themselves to be arranged in units according to their degree of interrelations", these units "correspond to the classes of the stylistic classification" (not so surprising) and "– as proved by the survivals – these units are characteristic of the successive chronological phases"[303]. In other words, the contexts are not used for a falsification of the typological and stylistic evidence, because the stylistic classification is used in the contextural analysis.

Thus Furumark's contribution to the study of Mycenaean pottery consists mainly of the development of a useful taxonomic system. He certainly added details to the chronological picture, but as his argumentation was evidently based on a "circulus vitiosus", it is not surprising that the general framework[304] based on stratigraphical evidence was still the only substantiated chronology for Mycenaean pottery – even after Furumark. Although several of Furumark's proposals thus remained hypothesis, they were not necessarily wrong however.

In the following I shall briefly summarize Furumark's considerations on the LH IIIC chronology of Rhodes. The system has not been adopted in the present study, but reference is frequently made to it.

Furumark on Rhodian chronology in the LH IIIC period

Rhodian material played a significant rôle in Furumark's chronological constructions, mainly because the excavations were to a great extent already published. In dealing with Rhodian material he considered Rhodian and Mainland[305] cultural development in LH III up to the first phase of IIIC to express more or less the same general tendencies (with certain specific types and divergent evolution on Rhodes). Except for LH IIIA2 this supposition has given rise to some misunderstandings. An excellent demonstration of Furumark's methods in relation to Rhodian material was given in his important article from 1944[306] where he proposed a tripartition of his LH IIIC:1 (in Rhodes and on the Mainland). His first phase was defined by the following characteristics : "a class of pottery decorated in what has been termed by me the "sub-IIIB" style"[307]. He then enumerates the "closed groups" for this period. To these pure "sub IIIB groups" should be added pottery contexts of this type which also included pottery of "distinctly different stylistic categories, the most conspicuous being the incipient Mainland Close Style and its Rhodian equivalents". This gave rise to the assumption that the first phase of IIIC was characterised by "sub-IIIB" and "incipient close style" – which has proved incorrect[308]. Furumark's chronology in this case is a good example of the above-mentioned typological argumentation. Apart from the fact that the Rhodian material was not published and excavated in a manner suited to more careful stratigraphi-

cal examination, evidently no attempt was made to do this as the find groups "allowed themselves to be arranged in units according to their degree of interrelation" and a fair number of "survivals" ensured the immediate succession from LH IIIB. The same types of typological and stylistic criteria are used to separate the next two phases. On the Mainland, LH IIIC:1b is the phase of the Granary at Mycenae and the "elaborated" close style, while Rhodes, now almost isolated from Mainland development, shows "a debased combination of the sub-IIIB class, characterized by a very poor decoration" and false-necked jars with cuttle-fish decoration. At the end of the phase, however, renewed Mainland influence makes itself felt on Rhodes[309]. This Mainland influence becomes very strong in the next phase, LH IIIC:1c, which is defined in the same way as "the continued evolution of the Mainland Close style", illustrating the transition to the simple decoration of the Submycenaean and Protogeometric periods[310].

New evidence for the chronology of the LH IIIB and IIIC periods

In the following I shall give a brief survey of the situation in the Western Aegean area, and comment upon the Levantine chronology as it appears following on more recent research, in an attempt to place Rhodian development in a relevant setting.

More recent studies in later Mycenaean chronology based on stratigraphical evidence from the Mainland and the Western Aegean have been published in several articles in later years. Well established chronological sequences for LH III have now been defined in Mycenae and Tiryns, Unterburg, in the Argolid[311] and from Lefkandi in Euboea[312]. J. Rutter took material earlier excavated from Korakou and Corinth, including material from Tiryns, Iria and elsewhere, as his basis and proposed a division into five of the LH IIIC period[313]. The material mentioned till here all derives from settlements, but Professor Iakovides succeeded in making a three-phase chronological framework for the late LH IIIB (?) – LH IIIC graves from Perati in Attica[314].

In the present connection it is important to emphasize the partition of LH IIIB into the IIIB1 and IIIB2 phases, separated by vast devastations (evidently earthquakes), as it becomes increasingly evident that this division reflects fundamental changes in the development of Mycenaean culture in the Argive centres (and to a certain extent even outside the Argolid). Recent excavations at Tiryns Unterburg proved that the great walls surrounding the Unterburg were erected in connection with the LH IIIB2 phase[315]. Moreover, newer work has demonstrated that the preceding fortification, in the LH IIIB1 phase, was probably more restricted and at any rate much less substantial[316]. At Mycenae most of the structures outside the citadel were destroyed towards the end of the LH IIIB1 phase and the bulk of material from IIIB2 was evidently found inside the citadel – the situation, however, is not quite clear. The division of IIIB was originally proposed by Professor Schachermeyr, who has now refined his subdivision into six chronological aspects, arranged in three main phases : Early IIIB, Middle IIIB and Late IIIB, the latest phase representing LH IIIB2[317]. Some of the main features in this subdivision were outlined by K. A. Wardle in 1973[318]. While the historical implications of the IIIB division in the Argolid seem fundamental even for cultural development outside the Argolid, the possibilities of distinguishing the two phases outside Mycenae and Tiryns have proved highly problematic. There seem two main reasons for this : 1) the distinction is based on "numerical analysis of total groups of material"[319]. Except for some specific "type fossil", it is difficult to separate the sherds of the two phases. 2) The division is based entirely on settlement material and it is impossible with certainty to classify grave groups within the IIIB2 phase.

Attempts to extend the IIIB2 phenomenon on the basis of definitions from Mycenae and Tiryns to other areas have met with little success – as pointed out. Thus Schachermeyr recently arrived at the rather pessimistic conclusion "so werden wir am besten tun, die Bezeichnung IIIB2 auf die Argolis und höchstens auch noch auf die Korinthia zu Beschränken"[320]. E. S. Sheratt, using the "Leitform's", "panelled pattern" and "rosette bowls" was able to include Laconia and Achaea, but maintained otherwise almost the same position as Schachermeyr[321]. In the Argolid it is tempting to suppose that several smaller villages ceased to be inhabited during the IIIB1 phase. In the IIIB2 phase the development towards a concentration around the major settlements, so clearly demonstrated in IIIC, might thus already have been in motion. Until more primary research is carried out in the field, this remains a hypothesis, however[321a]. Nevertheless, what we should conclude is that there exists a chronological phase in the Argolid in which the main characteristics are defined in a

way which evidently fails to allow a definition of a late IIIB phase in other areas. This does not, however, imply that the crucial events which obviously took place at the transition to IIIB2 had no influence on cultural development, and thus also on material culture elsewhere in the Mycenaean World – for instance in Rhodes. In spite of the difficulties in extending the concept of IIIB2 beyond the Argive settlement definitions, the term has sometimes been used in a broader sense. A case in point is Wulf Rudolf's treatment of the tombs from the Profitis Elias cemetery near Tiryns, in which the IIIB2 concept is extended to include tomb groups. The recently excavated material from the fortified hillside of Koukounaries in the Naoussa bay of Paros contains objects which to a certain degree are connected with the IIIB2 phase in the Argolid[322].

It is of great importance for the present investigations that a total change in cultural development is shown to have taken place in the Cycladic islands in the course of the LH IIIB period[323]. This phase was termed Late Cycladic III (Middle Phase) by Robin Barber and was supposed to last from mid LH IIIB to early LH IIIC. It is of significance that fortification systems were erected on several islands during the period and the direct contact and influence of mainland centres of Mycenaean power declined markedly[324]. As pointed out in the preceding chapter, a late IIIB phase on Rhodes as in the Cyclades should rather be synchronized with mid/late LH IIIB on the Mainland (in Schachermeyr's terms) than strictly with LH IIIB2.

Earlier in this chapter I outlined Arne Furumark's attempt to divide the LH IIIC period on Rhodes and in the Argolid into subphases. As pointed out by J. Rutter, it is rather instructive for the development of chronological studies in recent years that : "Desborough (following Furumark) considered the Close Style to be the earliest recognizable LH IIIC style in his 1964 study, and yet we are now discussing it as a feature of the *fourth* chronological stage within the ceramic development of the LH IIIC period"[325]. In this article J. Rutter distinguishes five stages in the development of pottery in LH IIIC, as was done by M. Popham and E. Milburn for the Lefkandi material[326]. The latest excavations at Tiryns, Unterburg, have demonstrated the existence of four distinct main phases : IIIC – früh, IIIC – entwickelt, III C – Fortgeschritten and IIIC – spät. Furthermore, a transitional LH IIIB/C phase has been defined[327]. The close style should be ascribed to phase IIIC – Fortgeschritten. Finally it should be mentioned that a continuous development into the Dark Ages has now been proved at Asine in the settlement area east of the Kastraki[328].

Cypriote chronology and the evidence of the historical events on Cyprus during the 13th and 12th centuries BC are somewhat contradictory. Even on this island the devastation on the Greek Mainland and the disorder this caused in society evidently interrupted contact with the Mycenaean centres in the Aegean[329]. The characteristic features of the Late Cypriote IIC phase are attested, among other places, at Maa-Palaeakastro on the westernmost coast of the island, Sinda (phase I), Kition (not least T.9 – upper stratum) and Enkomi. The pottery spectrum of this phase contains pottery of "Late Mycenaean IIIB" character, including shallow bowls with conical body and two horizontal strap handles at the rim, deep bowls with antithetic spiral pattern and kraters with decoration in "Rude Style"[330]. It has furthermore been suggested that Cretan exports to Cyprus increased and replaced Mycenaean products as a result of the weakening of power in Mainland centres[331].

A separate attitude was taken by Professor Schachermeyr, who considers the LC IIC/late LH IIIB phase to be the initial phase of the "Ashlar Towns"[332]. The pottery of the "late LH IIIB" period in Cyprus is almost exclusively locally made, and in my opinion contains elements which should rather be dated in early IIIC according to Aegean classification. We thus have to consider the possibility that the LC IIC phase in reality is contemporary with both late LH IIIB and early IIIC in the Argive sense of classification.

The transition to the Late Cypriote IIIA phase seems obscure, and – as in the Aegean – it seems difficult to define a clear borderline between pottery of LC IIC/Late Myc. IIIB and LC IIIA/early Myc. IIIC character. The evidence from Enkomi is not without ambiguity. The detailed chronology for the LC III period (with a majority of locally produced pottery) is still to a great extent based on Aegean evidence as elaborated by Furumark. At present, thus, Cypriote connections during the 12th century BC can only exceptionally be instructive for Aegean chronology.

A note on Southern Rhodes in the LH IIIA2 to IIIC periods

The most recent studies of Late Mycenaean Rhodes were carried out by C. Mee[333]. In his chapter on the Ialysos cemeteries Mee provides quite a substantial discussion of Rhodian pottery chronology. It is actually characteristic of Rhodes that there is virtually no stratigraphical information and that the island shows rather specific, local features in the pottery. It must thus be underlined that the chronological proposals in the previous chapters are only proposals : in several cases they may be altered when new information comes to hand. In the following I should like to sum up some of the results of the present study – results which may add some additional dimensions to the various studies made by Mee.

LH IIIA2/early IIIB. In the material treated above it has been almost impossible to distinguish pottery of the early IIIB period. It should be remembered that even in the Argolid the transition is vague. Zygouries kylikes do actually occur, not least at several sites in southern Rhodes[334], but the early type of A-skyphoi does not with certainty[335]. It has been suggested that there was less of a contrast between III A2 and B in southern Rhodes[336], but, as pointed out by Mee, a detailed estimation of such an element of conservatism must await further excavations. LH IIIA2, on the other hand, seems well defined in Ialysos, and in southern Rhodes the earlier pottery from Passia grave 1 and, first and foremost, the pottery from Granto, Kattavia, perfectly fits the traditional definition of the phase. At the present stage of knowledge an occupation of the Kattavia area later than LH IIIA2 is based on very few and rather doubtful testimonies[337].

On the basis of spectrographic analysis of samples from Ialysos, Jones and Mee recently concluded that the majority of the LH IIIA2 pottery from Rhodes was imported from the Argolid[338]. In spite of the local styles so often emphasized for Rhodes in the period concerned[339], quite an amount of Rhodian IIIA2 pottery actually fits a theory of Argive provenance, and I am much inclined to agree that fairly large quantities were imported to Rhodes, even to the southern part of the island.

Late LH IIIB. The development in LH IIIB on Rhodes is rather obscure. In 1975 Mee proposed that relations between the Argolid and the Dodecanese diminished considerably or almost

113

vanished during the LH III B2 phase. Stirrup jar types FS 167, 170, 173 and 179 et al., should be imported and be dated within the IIIB1 phase, while stirrup jars of type FS 182 (as 4,7 supra) should be dated in III B2, thus being locally made. Mee's dissertation furthermore contained the supposition that "at Ialysos the patterned kylix continued in use throughout III B – in the Argolid, of course, there are none in III B2"[340]. In the previously mentioned article from 1978, Jones and Mee analysed 17 LH IIIB pots out of which just two were local, the rest being imported partly from the Argolid, partly from elsewhere in the Greek World (Boeotia, Attica, East Crete/Naxos). The changing import pattern well fits a theory of a less productive and less forceful commercial development in the Argolid in IIIB, as indicated by the changes on the plain during LH IIIB. Finally, in 1982, Mee gave up the attempt to divide the Rhodian IIIB into two phases. He did, however, suggest that "stagnation set in because the influence of the Peloponnese diminished as the period progressed", and he even believed "that Ialysos and possibly a number of other sites on the northwest coast were destroyed during the course of LH IIIB"[341]. As pointed out by Mee himself, this picture is admittedly difficult to prove at the present stage of our knowledge. Nonetheless what should be emphasized is that the value of the concept of a so-called "III B koiné style" is highly doubtful, both when used for classification and when considering the political, social and commercial realities behind that concept.

In the present study Passia grave 4 is considered to represent a late phase of LH IIIB on Rhodes. The grave contained an example of the carinated stirrup jar FS 182 (Passia 4,7) with circumcurrent quirk and the later development of the painted kylix (Passia 4,4). This type of stirrup jar is widely distributed in the Aegean and Eastern Mediterranean – and it does not seem local. The decorated jug with the bird (Passia 4,2) was stylistically connected with the Cypriote "rude" or "pastoral" style, and the heavy piriform (globular) shape of the jar Passia 4,5 was likewise related to Cypriote fabrics. It is interesting to note that the transformed Mycenaean "Rude Style" in this way has been re-exported back to the Aegean. The deep bowl Passia 4,3 seems to belong to the chronological horizon when Cretan pottery was under the influence of the late Mycenaean IIIB Mainland. The rest of the pottery from Passia grave 4 seems more or less local – of specific interest is the krater Passia 4,8.

It is hardly necessary to emphasize that the elements defined constitute only a very vague basis for a definition of late IIIB on Rhodes. It is likewise not at all evident how such a phase could be defined in Ialysos – probably at least the FS 182 stirrup jars with circumcurrent quirk from Ialysos OT A should be included. Cypriote influence in the Aegean is neither restricted to Rhodes nor to the LH IIIB phase. It is important to point out, however, that such influence does actually occur in IIIB2 even on the Mainland[342]. Moreover, if the Cape Gelidonya shipwreck is rightly dated around 1200 B.C., the evidence increases considerably[343].

The influence of the changed social and political conditions at the transition between LH IIIB1 and IIIB2 on the Mainland and the Cycladic islands, on the rest of the Mycenaean World, was probably fundamental. If the previously mentioned results of Jones and Mee can be considered to be of general value, it seems as if the pattern of trade with Rhodes changed already before the transition to LH IIIB2 in the Argolid – a dominating Argive import pattern gave way to a more composite one where other areas of the Mycenaean World also participated in the trade. It is hardly astonishing that this alteration in the pattern of trade resulted in some influence from Cyprus, which enjoyed a considerable reinforcement of relations with the Aegean around the transition to the LH IIIC period – leading to an actual colonization of Cyprus.

LH IIIC early/mid and late

In the previously mentioned article by Jones and Mee, 17 out of 22 IIIC samples were local[344]. The octopus stirrup jar from Ialysos NT 84,6, considered by the late Dr. Desborough to be Cretan inspired or imported, proved in fact to be imported[345]. Besides this jar, which was found in a rather early IIIC context, Cretan imports in my opinion are astonishingly rare in Mycenaean Rhodes. As to the local octopus stirrup jars, it is worth noting that they are all found in the northern part of the island – mainly in Ialysos – never in the southern. The LH IIIC phenomenon termed the "Aegean koiné" by V. d'A. Desborough mainly refers to these jars which are to be considered rather late in the Rhodian IIIC development. In this more advanced stage of IIIC on Rhodes there undoubtedly seems to be a growing tendency towards more contact with the outside world – but it seems difficult to prove that even the early IIIC reusers of the tombs in

114

Ialysos and Kalavarda-Kamiros actually were newcomers[346]. As pointed out by Mee, the differences between the northern and southern part of the island are considerable[347]. Whether this factor expresses the differences between the dominating, but furthermore rather specific site of Ialysos and the surroundings, or actually embodies fundamental cultural divergences between the north and the south part of the island, can only be judged through future excavations.

In the present study I propose a division of the LH IIIC period into two parts, based on the successive burials in Passia grave 1, a division which might only in part be extended to the northern area of the island. The vertical zigzag patterns and triangular chevron pattern on open bowls with vertical handles on the rim, spherical jugs, and biconical jars are rather characteristic of the early phase. Relations with this group are found in Astypalia and Langada, Kos – showing that the development in southern Rodes is not isolated, but is rather an element of a Dodecanesian development. The rest of the pottery from the early IIIC phase, undoubtedly mainly local, shows more or less close relations with LH IIIB predecessors.

The middle and/or late phase is only defined by three pieces – which, on the other hand, show greater affinity with Ialysos than the former group. This is primarily demonstrated by the deep bowl Passia 1,11 with its exact counterpart in Ialysos NT 17 – the central pattern in the antithetic spiral panel is found so widely dispersed as in Acrocorinth and Tarsus. The shape of the stirrup jar Passia 1,12 resembles that of the characteristic octopus stirrup jars in northern Rhodes, and the stemmed spirals, isolated or in an antithetic composition, are likewise found in Ialysos. A middle/late IIIC phase including the majority of the octopus stirrup jars and related material could undoubtedly be isolated in Ialysos.

It should thus be emphasized that, at least in southern Rhodes but probably even in larger parts of the Dodecanese, the transition to LH IIIC is *not* marked by the arrival of newcomers. Such a migration should rather be related to the above-mentioned advanced stage of LH IIIC. In terms of relative chronology the early phase of IIIC should probably be contemporary with Troy VIh, shown by Chr. Podzuweit to be contemporary with early IIIC on the Mainland. The advanced stage should be paralleled more or less with Troy VIIa[348].

The existence of tassel motifs and inscribed triangles on the upper part of closed jars from Apsaktiras and Asklepio might indicate an influence from the Western Aegean in a phase contemporary with LH IIIC Fortgeschritten – Spät in Tiryns, the Lion Gate X deposit in Mycenae, Lefkandi 2b/3 et al.[349]. Thus Furumark was probably right concerning the significant Mainland influence on Rhodes in the latest phase of LH IIIC.

A Post-Mycenaean period?

Only two vases could be dated in a Post-Mycenaean phase not yet possible to call Protogeometric. The large stirrup jar 12502 should be considered a representative of the renewed Cypriote connection in the Aegean that is shown to have taken place after the termination of LH IIIC[350].

This is the period of the Alaas cemetery in Cyprus. Perhaps it is significant that this jar was found in the vicinity of Lindos where the earlier development in the Dark Ages could have been strongest. Considering the decoration of the Submycenaean stirrup jar 12501, it seems to be related to the Submycenaean material defined from Miletus and elsewhere on the west coast of Anatolia.

115

Notes

Preface

1. *Fouilles de Vroulia*, Berlin 1914.
2. *ActaA* 28, 1957, pp. 1–192.
3. A brief treatment of the history of the expedition is given in S. Dietz and S. Trolle, *Arkæologens Rhodos*, København 1974.
4. *Lindos, Fouilles de l'Acropole 1902–1914 et 1952*, Berlin/Copenhagen 1960.

Introduction

5. *Mee 1982*.

A. Catalogue of graves, grave goods and survey material

6. *BMCat Glass* I, p. 45 ff, G – "Curls of Hair".
7. *BMCat Glass* I, p. 41 ff.
8. *BMCat Glass* I, no. 53.
9. *Prosymna*, Fig. 599,7.
10. *BSA* 68, 1973, p. 147.
11. cit. p. 147.
12. *BSA* 68, 1973, p. 147 f.
13. *Chamber Tombs*, T 518, 68, d.
14. *Chamber Tombs*, T 518, 68, e.
15. *Chamber Tombs*, T 518, 67.
16. *Chamber Tombs*, T 523, 10.
17. *Chamber Tombs*, Pl. VIII, T 518, 67.
18. A. Maiuri, *ASAtene* 6–7, Fig. 157.

B. Chronology and discussion

19. G. Konstantinoupoulos, *AAA*, 6, 1973, p. 124, Fig. 13. The material was kindly shown to me by Miss Olga Sachariadhou in Rhodes.
20. *Deltion*, 26 (1971), p. 551. Hope Simpson R. and J. F. Lazenby, *BSA* 68, 1973, p. 161 and *Gazetteer*, p. 364.
21. Heraklion Museum, inv. no. 3644. I am indebted to Chr. Podzuweit for this reference. Another Cretan specimen, rather close to the Lachania piece, is from Gournes gr. 4, *Kanta, LM III*, Pl. 21,10 – LM IIIB.
22. *French IV*, p. 153, Fig. 3.
23. C. W. Blegen et al., *Troy Settlements VIIa, VIIb and VIII*. Vol. IV, Connecticut 1958, Pls. 225 and 249, no. 33,172. Chr. Podzuweit proposes Troy VIIa to be dated rather late in the LH IIIC development. "Die Mykenische Welt und Troja", *Prähistorische Archäologie in Südosteuropa* Bd. 1, Berlin 1982 p. 80.
24. *Mee 1982*, pp. 30–31.

25. *BMCat* 1,1, A925 and *CVA* Brit. 7,21.
26. *Mee 1982*, p. 34.
27. *Perati*, p. 77 Dating : per. 1–2.
28. Voigtländer W. *AAA* 6, 1973, p. 37. Abb. 9.
29. *MP*, p. 339 and *Furumark IIIC*, p. 198. Semicircles in a triangular patch are often found in the handle zone of stirrup jars, *MP*, p. 338.
30. *CVA* DK, Pl. 50, 1–7.
31. A. Maiuri, *ASAtene*, 6–7, Fig. 79,10.
32. *Mee 1982*, p. 18. In LH IIIA2 context from Mycenae, *French II*, p. 188.
33. *French V* (Perseia trench), p. 74.
34. *BCH* 89, 1965, p. 716, Fig. 20.
35. E. French, K. A. Wardle and D. Wardle, *Type Chart*.
36. *Furumark IIIC*, p. 207.
37. *Tiryns* 1978/79, Abb. 56.6 – "Frühes SH IIIC".
38. G. Jacobi, *ASAtene* 13–14, p. 339, Fig. 88 – dated by C. Mee to the LH IIIB phase. It is, however, a rather atypical FS 192 piece and LH IIIC is probably a more correct dating.
39. L. Morricone, *ASAtene* NS 34–35, 1972–73, p. 352 Fig. 345, g.
40. *Mee 1982*, passim. *Stubbings Levant*, p. 15.
41. For instance, Ialysos gr. XXVII, A. Maiuri, *ASAtene*, 6–7, p. 155, Fig. 79, no. 5.
42. E.g. French I, Pl. 70 (d), 4.
43. *Mee 1982*, Table 2 ff.
44. Perati phase 2, *Perati 3*, Pl. 34.
45. Inv. no. 8696, no provenance, purchased in Rome in 1927 by Chr. Blinkenberg from F. Benedetti, Via del Babuino. Said to be from Greece.
46. L. Morricone, *ASAtene*, NS 27–28, Fig. 21, b.
47. *Kanta, LM III*, Pl. 118,7.
48. *BMCat* 1,1, A 1016 from Kalymnos, *BMCat* 1,2, Abb. 72, 203 for Cyprus. See also Passia 1,2 supra for motif.
49. *CVA* DK, Pl. 59,3, dated in *Mee 1982* in the LH IIIB period (like Furumark) on poor dating premises – FS 183.
50. Th. Papadopoulos, *Mycenaean Achaea*, 1978/79, no. 4086.
51. *French Tarsus*, p. 58, Fig. 4,2–3.
52. *Perati* no. 141, gr. 9 (per. 1-2).
53. L. Morricone, *ASAtene* NS 27–28, gr. 22 (inv.no. 261), p. 143 Fig. 130, gr. 60, p. 263, Fig. 294 (probably early LH IIIC).
54. *CVA* DK, Pl. 44,3–4.
55. *CVA* DK, Pl. 44,5.
56. *CVA* DK, Pl. 45,1–2.
57. *MP*, FS 148.
58. Cit. p. 209, note 4.

59. Cit. p. 220, note 3.
60. *Mee 1982*, p. 148.
61. *Mee 1982*, Pl. 13,1.
62. *MPVP*, XII, 17.
63. *Furumark IIIC*, p. 219.
64. "Decorazione a fasce segmenti a doppio spina de pesce...". A. Maiuri, *ASAtene* 6–7, Fig. 157 (3448).
65. *Mee 1982*, p. 142.
66. For instance, in the famous "IIIC early" grave 48 from Kalavarda, Aniforos ("Kamiros"). *CIRh*, VI-VII, p. 144, Fig. 169 – *Furumark IIIC* : LH IIIC:1a and *Desborough 1964*, p. 6.
67. L. Morricone, *ASAtene* NS 27–28, p. 74, Fig. 46.
68. L. Morricone, *ASAtene* NS 27–28, p. 261, Fig. 290. The grave is transitional IIIB/C or very early LH IIIC.
69. *CVA* DK, Pl. 41,6 (Apollakia), Pl. 42,4 ("Rhodes").
70. A. Maiuri, *ASAtene* 6–7, Fig. 43,55. *Mee 1982*, Pl. 38.
71. I was able to study the bowl in the Rhodes Museum in September 1982.
72. *Ialysos NT* 61, inv.no. 12593.
73. *Furumark IIIC*, p. 207.
74. *Lefkandi*, p. 340 and Fig. 4,1. The feature is usual on Submycenaean deep bowls from Kerameikos.
75. J. Rutter, *Hesperia* 48:4, 1979, Fig. 5,9 and Pl. 91,9.
76. *French, Tarsus*, p. 60, Fig. 10, 1299.
77. *JFA* Vol. 5, 1978, p. 466.
78. See *Mee 1982*, p. 32 ff.
79. *Mee 1982*, Pl. 30.3.
80. G. Jacopi, *ASAtene* 13–14. p. 290, Fig. 34.
81. *Furumark IIIC*, p. 198 and p. 203.
82. Compare W. Cavanagh and C. Mee, *BSA* 73, 1978, p. 38.
83. *BMCat* 1,1, A 1011.
84. G. Jacopi, *ASAtene*, 13–14, p. 339, Fig. 87 (centre).
85. Perati 2, p. 265, stirrup jar from grave 8 (phase 1 and 2).
86. W. Cavanagh and C. Mee, *BSA* 73, 1978, p. 31 ff. with additions and corrigenda by M. Benzi, *SMEA*, 23, 1982, p. 323 ff.
87. W. Cavanagh and C. Mee cit. p. 42.
88. *CVA* DK 59,19 and 60,12.
89. Mee 1982, p. 149.
90. E.g. *French* II, p. 54, (a), 5.
91. *CVA* DK, Pl. 56,4.
92. *Mee 1982*, p. 144.
93. Th. G. Spyropoulos, *Praktika* 1979, (1981), p. 33 and Pl. 18.
94. *Prosymna*, Fig. 572 – LH IIIA2 grave.
95. L. Morricone, *ASAtene* NS 27–28, no. 10, p. 62 and Fig. 30. The grave contained at least LH IIIA2 and LH IIIC pottery.
96. Cit. no. 4, Fig. 47. LH IIIC grave.
97. Cit. no. 3, Fig. 131. The six vases preserved seem to indicate a dating in early LH IIIC (and late IIIB ?).
98. Cit. no. 3, Fig. 284. Three burials covering the period LH IIIA2 – IIIC, compare the above mentioned Tanagra context.
99. L. Morricone, *ASAtene* NS 34–35, p. 38, Fig. 38 and Fig. 379.
100. For instance, *Tiryns* 1976, Abb. 29,3 and *Tiryns* 1977, Abb. 37,5.
101. Compare *Ialysos* NT 83, 6B (=12765). G. Jacopi, *ASAtene* 13–14, Fig. 63, and supra Passia 1,2.
102. *Asine* I, Fig. 249,8 – dated LH IIIC:1a according to *Furumark IIIC*, p. 197.
103. L. Morricone, *ASAtene* NS 27–28, Fig. 196,d. p. 191.
104. *Mee 1982*, pp. 16,24 and 41.

105. N. K. Sandars, *AJA* 67, 1963, p. 153 ff. and p. 150 ff. H. W. Catling, *BSA* 63, 1968, p. 95 ff.
106. D. Theocharis, AAA 1, p. 293, Fig. 2 (Type F ii). Late 12th century BC.
107. E. MacNamara, *ProcPS* 36, 1970, p. 241, Fig. 1.
108. L. Morricone, *ASAtene* NS 34–35, 1972–73, p. 253, Figs. 198 and 199. Compare the piece from Zapher Papoura, N. K. Sandars, *AJA* 67, 1963. Pl. 25,32.
109. Another specimen said to be from Rhodes is cited in O. Montelius La Grèce Préclass. 1924, Pl. 13,1.
110. Th. G. Spyropoulos, Ὑστερομυκηναικοί ελλαδικοι θησαυροί, Athen 1972, p. 159 ff. H. W. Catling is inclined to place them later than 1200 BC., *BSA* 63, 1968, p. 96.
111. L. Morricone, *ASAtene* NS 27–28, p. 214–215, Figs. 226–227.
112. L. Morricone, *ASAtene* NS 27–28, p. 238 ff.
113. *Perati*, Pl. 82, (phase 3).
114. L. Morricone, *ASAtene* NS 27–28, p. 102, Fig. 82.
115. See also Ialysos NT 70,15 (LH IIIC).
116. Compare also Apsaktiras nos. 9–10, infra p.
117. N.K. Sandars *ProcPS* 20, 1955, p. 175 ff. and cit. pp. 188–190. H. W. Catling, *BSA* 63, 1968, p. 107.
118. A. Maiuri, *ASAtene* 6–7, Fig. 106.
119. See also *Mee 1982*, p. 129 f.
120. *ASAtene* NS 27–28, p. 57, Fig. 29.
121. Cit. p. 214, Fig. 231.
122. G. Cadogan, *BSA* 62, 1967, p. 261, Fig. 2,8 and Pl. 48 (solid black inside – LM IIIC). H. W. Catling, *BSA* 63, 1968, p. 115 – late type LM IIIC/(LH IIIC2). M. Popham, *BSA* 65, 1970, Pl. 47,e (from Little Palace).
123. No 200, P. Åström et al. *SIMA* XLV :1, Pl. 78, 200. V. Karageorghis, *Acts Nicosia* 1978, Pl. XXV,5.
124. *Barbouna* 2, no. 111, p. 82 – proposed dating : LH IIIB2.
125. Tiryns 1977, p. 420, Abb. 40 – from early IIIC.
126. R. Felsch in R. Hägg and N. Marinatos, *Sanctuaries and Cults in the Aegean Bronze Age*, Sthlm. 1981, p. 85 Abb. 4.
127. K. A. Wardle, *BSA* 64, 1969, p. 277, Fig. 7,76.
128. p. 101.
129. *CVA* DK Pl. 39,6.
130. *MPVP* XIII,5, p. 168.
131. *BMCat* 1,1 A 879. *MV* Pl. IX, 58.
132. A. Maiuri, *ASAtene* 6–7, p. 108, Fig. 113.
133. *Chamber Tombs* pl. 47,9.
134. *Zygouries* T. 33,2 Fig. 166 and Pl. XIX.
135. *Deiras*, p. 153.
136. *French* V, p. 73.
137. D. Anson, *OpusAth* XIII, 1980, p. 4 and Fig. 2.
138. *MPVP*, p. 63 ff.
139. Anson cit., p. 14 ff., earlier however in *MPVP*, and V. Karageorghis, *Cyprus from the Stone Age to the Romans*, 1982, p. 86 and 110. The "rude style" as such, covers the time span LC IIC to early LC IIIA. See also infra p. 113.
140. *MPVP* XI, 121 = *MV*, Pl. XXXVIII,384.
141. For instance, Ialysos NT 83,1 G. Jacopi, *ASAtene* 13–14. p. 315, Fig. 62 – the grave being a type grave of Furumark's IIIC:1c.
142. L. Morricone, *ASAtene* NS 34–35, p. 375, Fig. 375. Also *Ägäische Frühzeit* IV, Tf. 28, p. 149.
143. Or late IIIB/early IIIC, see infra note 151, D. Schilardi, *Praktika* 1977, p. 368, Pl. 190 x.
144. *Tiryns* 1978/79, p. 474.
145. *Tiryns* 1978/79, Abb. 48,4, with antithetic spirals.
146. *Tiryns* 1977, Abb. 39,10, Abb. 40,7 and Abb. 42,7.
147. *Ägäische Frühzeit* III, p. 88 f. and Abb. 16 – likewise with rather deep band.

117

148. *Tiryns* 1976, Abb. 29,14, Tiryns 1978/79, Abb. 48,4.
149. *Ägäische Frühzeit* II, in "3. Aspekt" (House of the Idols), but not later.
150. *Lefkandi*, p. 347, Fig. 8,5.
151. D. U. Schilardi in J. L. Davis and J. F. Cherry, *Papers in Cycladic Prehistory*, Los Angeles 1979, p. 160, Fig. 18.
152. *Ägäische Frühzeit* II, pp. 287–288. According to F. Schachermeyr, skyphoi are not found in Cyprus until this phase, *Ägäische Frühzeit* III, p. 172 et al. A comment on Schachermeyr's Cypriot Chronology is found infra on p. 113.
153. *Enkomi IIIa*, Pl. 67,27, Pl. 70,25 and Pls. 71,73,18,19,21,22 and 27, Pl. 123, 10, 12, 13.
154. *Kition* I, pp. 93–94 and Pl. LXXII. V. Karageorghis, *Cyprus from the Stone Age to the Romans*, Lond. 1982, pp. 84–85.
155. *French* IV, p. 183. Zygouries kylikes however are found even in early LH IIIC contexts in Tiryns, *Tiryns* 1978/79, p. 208.
156. C. Mee, *The Dodecanese in the Bronze Age*, p. 103.
157. Chr. Podzuweit, *JRGZM* 26, 1979, p. 206, Abb. 19,1 dated LH IIIB1.
158. *Chamber Tombs* T 502,13 – FS 40.
159. For shape, see *Enkomi* IIIa, Pl. 112, 1978/5 and Pl. 196,18 – the handles however are placed higher.
160. *Nouveaux Documents*, p. 219.
161. *MPVP*, V, 61, p. 51. *Kition* I, Pl. 56, no. 134 (Tomb 9, house burial), C. F. A. Shaeffer, *Ugaritica* II, 1949, p. 225, Fig. 94, C (kratér ?).
162. *Tiryns* 1978/79, Abb. 56,9.
163. O. Broneer, *Hesperia* 8, 1939, Fig. 45,6.
164. L. Morricone, *ASAtene* NS 27–28, p. 258, Fig. 284 (inv. no. 237).
165. L. Morricone, *ASAtene* NS 43–44, T. 59, 46 and 36.
166. *Mee 1982*, p. 23.
167. *CVA* DK, Pl. 58.
168. *Mee 1982*, p. 24.
169. *BMCat* 1,1 A 904.
170. R. E. Jones and C. Mee, *JFA* 5,4, 1978, p. 461 ff.
171. *Tiryns* VI, p. 102.
172. *Zygouries*, Fig. 131, Fig. 137,6 and Pl. XVI,1. Also, *Ägäische Frühzeit* II, p. 251, Abb. 52.
173. C. F. A. Schaeffer, *Ugaritica* VII, Paris 1972, Fig. 36,3, p. 307.
174. *BMCat* 1,1, A 1070,2. On dating : *French* V, p. 71, note 4.
175. Verdelis et al., *Deltion* 20, A 1965, p. 146, Fig. 5,2. As far as I understand, this stirrup jar was considered late LH IIIB by Voigtländer, *Tiryns* VI, pp. 251–252, note 44.
176. Verdelis et al., *Deltion* 20 A, 1965, p. 140, Fig. 1,5.
177. *Tiryns* 1977, abb. 37,11, *Tiryns* 1978/79, Abb. 56,7.
178. *Tiryns* 1976, Abb. 35,13.
179. *JHS-AR* 28, 1981–82, p. 22, Fig. 43.
180. *French* IV, Fig. 11,13, no. 90.
181. Also *Ägäische Frühzeit* II, p. 253 f. Note that no example of this pattern was found in the LH IIIB1 deposit inside the Citadel, published by K. A. Wardle, *BSA* 64, 1969.
182. From the "Causeway deposit", K. A. Wardle, *BSA 68, p. 316, Fig. 11, 81* and the *"Perseia Trench"*, *French* V, Fig. 7,5 (probably band-shaped).
183. *BMCat* 1,1 A 903, also MV II,9.
184. G. Jacopi, *ASAtene* 13–14, Fig. 61 (12763) and Fig. 65 (12778).
185. *Furumark IIIC*, p. 198.
186. For the octopus jar, see R. E. Jones and C. Mee, *JFA* 5,4, 1978, p. 469 (no. 35).

187. C. F. A. Schaeffer, *Ugaritica* II, Paris 1949, Fig. 64, (9), p. 165.
188. Verdelis et al., *Deltion* 20, A, Fig. 5,1 and p. 143 (probably FS 9).
189. D. U. Schilardi, in J. L. Davis and J. F. Cherry, *Papers in Cycladic Prehistory*, Los Angeles 1979, p. 167, Fig. 8 and *Ergon* 1977, p. 149, Fig. 97. On the dating of Koukounaries see further infra p. 112.
190. L. Morricone, *ASAtene* NS 34–35. 1972–73, p. 358 ff.
191. Dated by him to LH IIIA2 and IIIB, *Mee 1982*, p. 17 and 25 – according to this auther no IIIC kraters at all were found on Rhodes (in graves) – see supra *1,4*.In settlement material, however, kraters are probably well represented during this phase, infra p. 103.
192. *CVA* DK, Pl. 49, 3–5.
193. G. Jacopi, *ASAtene* 13–14, p. 338.
194. Supra p. 60ff.
195. *CVA* DK, Pl. 49,4 – for a related pattern from Aegina, S. Hiller, *Alt Ägina* IV,1, "Mykenische Keramik", Mainz 1975, no. 363, dated by Hiller in LH IIIB:1.
196. *Zygouries* Pl. XVIII.
197. C. F. A. Schaeffer, *Ugaritica* VII, Paris 1978, p. 345, Fig. 53,2, dated around 1230 B.C.
198. *Tiryns* 1976, Abb. 27,10 related krater motifs from "Seraglio", Kos, L. Morricone, *ASAtene* NS 34–35, p. 375, Fig. 375 et al.
199. For instance *MPVP* V, 1–2.
200. A. Maiuri, *ASAtene* 6–7, p. 56, Fig. 60,11.
201. See infra Passia *4,10*.
202. *Mee 1982*, p. 25.
203. *French* III-V, passim.
204. *MP* p. 285 – but with a shorter stamen. *French* II, p. 177, Pl. 51, (c), 5.
205. French and Wardle cit. passim.
206. *MP* p. 451 and *Mee 1982*, p. 88.
207. L. Morricone, *ASAtene* NS 34–35, p. 287, Fig. 253.
208. Compare also the deep semiglobular side-spouted cup, Passia *2,2* supra.
209. *ASAtene* NS 27–28, p. 21 (inv.no. 188) and Fig. 232.
210. Supra p. 99.
211. On the Mainland not found until Rutter's phase 4, J. Rutter, *Symposium on the Dark Ages in Greece*, N.Y. 1977, p. 4. In Tiryns only from LH IIIC entwickelt (Chr. Podzuweit personal communication).
212. L. Morricone, *ASAtene* NS 27–28, p. 227, Fig. 245, (inv.no. 197).
213. Supra p. 56. Fig. 60.
214. E. French, *BSA* 66, 1971, p. 131 ff.
215. W. Cavanagh and C. Mee, *BSA* 73, 1978, p. 42.
216. E. French cit. p. 131 ff.
217. E. French cit. p. 132.
218. *JGS* X, 1968, pp. 9–16.
219. See also *BMCat Glass* I, Pl. IV and Fig. 3, 56, subtype G, IV.
220. Yalouris *JGS* X, 1968, p. 12.
221. Th. J. Papadopoulos, *Mycenaena Achaea*, 1978/79, p. 141 (PMX 12), p. 199 and Fig. 291 (a).
222. A. Maiuri, *ASAtene* 6–7, p. 57, Fig. 61.
223. L. Morricone, *ASAtene* NS 27–28, p. 179, Fig. 189.
224. For instance, *Prosymna*, Fig. 599,8.
225. R. Barber, *BSA* 76, 1981, p. 11. "Late Cycladic III (Middle Phase)".
226. *French* IV, Fig. 12,46 and K. A. Wardle, *BSA* 64, Fig. 6,50. The deep bowl with antithetic spirals depicted by Wardle was considered to be Middle IIIB according to Schachermeyr, *Ägäische Frühzeit* II, p. 251, Fig. 55, *Ägäische Frühzeit* IV, p. 43, Abb. 2. For Schachermeyr's opinion see further infra p. 112.

227. M. R. Popham, BSA 60, 1965, p. 322, Fig. 3,1 dated early LM IIIC.
228. *Mee* 1982, p. 148.
229. *Mee* 1982, p. 149.
230. Supra Fig. 50, and supra p. 49.
231. *Asine* I, Fig. 240. Several pieces are naturally found in earlier contexts.
232. N. K. Sandars, *ProcPS* 20, 1955, pp. 174–197.
233. J. Boardman, *The Cretan Collection in Oxford, The Dictaean Cave and the Iron Age Crete*, Oxford 1961, p. 20, Fig. 4,70.
234. *JRGZM* 2, 1955, p. 156 – also from Kos, L. Morricone, *ASAtene* NS 34–35, p. 278 f. (no. 3), Fig. 239 (Sandar's 1b type).
235. Vl. Milojcic, *JRGZM* 2, 1955, p. 155, Abb. 1,2.
236. G. Despini, *Praktika* 1979 (1981), Pl. 143 and pp. 232–235 mentioning traits of LH IIIA2 and IIIC character – in my opinion the pieces depicted well fit a IIIB dating.
237. Maiuri, *ASAtene* 6–7, p. 149, Fig. 147.
238. *Mee* 1982, p. 133 f.
239. A. Maiuri, *ASAtene* 6–7, p. 67, Fig. 70.
240. *Mee* 1982, p. 128.
241. *AJA* 67, p. 140 ff, see also the same author in *The Sea Peoples, Warriors of the Ancient Mediterranean*, London 1978, p. 158, Figs. 106–110.
242. *Mee* 1982, p. 106, Siana-Kymisala, note 5.
243. *MV*, Tf. D.9, *Mee* 1982, p. 60.
244. I. Zervoudaki, *Deltion* 26, (1971), Pl. 559, p. 550 ff.
245. This piece was shown to me by Miss Olga Zachariadou, who also kindly showed me the pottery from the grave, which covers the following periods : early and Late IIIA, early and late IIIB, early and middle late IIIC.
246. Supra p. 101 infra p. 114.
247. Infra p. 108.
248. Th. G. Spyropoulos, Υστερομυκηναικοί ελλαδικοι θησαυροι Ath. 1972, Pl. 27,
249. S. Marinatos, *Archaeologia Homerica* I, A. p. 16 ff. S. Iakovidis, *BSA* 72, pp. 113–119.
250. *MPVP* IV, 41, with references.
251. F. Biancofiore, *La Civiltá Micenea nell'Italia Meridionale*, Roma 1963, Pl. XVI, 154.
252. K. A. Wardle, *BSA* 64, 1969, p. 271, Fig. 5,22.
253. *CVA* DK Pl. 42,6, with provenance "Rhodes".
254. For instance, O. Broneer, *Hesperia* 8, Fig. 35, p. 359, from the Athenian Acropolis, attributed by Rutter to his first phase, *Symposium on the Dark Ages in Greece*, N.Y. 1977, p. 2. The reserved type from Acrocorinth however in phases 3–5. J. Rutter, *Hesperia* 48, sherd no. 7 – these are all of the shape FM 43,38.
255. *Prehistoric Emporio*, no. 2744. Evidently referring to Rutter's chronological system corresponding to Lefkandi 2b. For the pattern see also C. W. Blegen et al. *Troy* III, 2, Pl. 421,23 and Ialysos, G. Jacopi, *ASAtene* 13–14, 1933. (gr. LXVI), p. 275 et al.
256. I am greatly indebted to Chr. Podzuweit who drew my attention to this piece. Furthermore a mug (FS 226) with the same pattern was found in the Epichosis.
257. *Prehistoric Emporio*, p. 582, no. 2700.
258. *MP*, FS 35, 32 – see also *Mee* 1982, p. 72, who considers it rather to be of shape FS 37.
259. *MP* p. 389.
260. Tiryns 1981, p. 392, also note 259 and Abb. 16,1. Note also the motif on a SM stirrup jar from Nauplia, C.-G. Styrenius, *Submycenaean Studies*, Fig. 51. A similar motif on a closed-shape jar from Asine was dated by Barbro Santillo Frizell in her final Mycenaean phase, *Asine* II, 3, no. 496.

261. Treated in connection with Passia 1,1, 1,8 and 1,10.
262. L. Morricone, *ASAtene* NS 34–35, Figs. 252, 371 and 373.
263. In Tiryns characteristic of the LH IIIC Fortgeschritten bis Spät, *Tiryns* 1981, p. 390 and Figs 12,2 – 14,7.
264. *CVA* DK, passim.
265. Latest *Mee* 1982, pp. 67–71.
266. Infra p. 110.
267. *Mee* 1982, p. 69.
268. p. 97, note 49.
269. See supra.
270. White paint like this was found in Tiryns during the LH IIIC early phase – not later.
271. R. Hope Simpson and R. Lazenby, *BSA* 68, 1973, p. 150.
272. For a similar motif, see A. Maiuri, *ASAtene* 6–7, p. 174, Fig. 160 (3426), also from el-Amarna, *BMCat* 1,1 A 997,1.
273. *Chamber Tombs* T. 520, Pl. XVII, 16.
274. *CVA* DK, Pl. 59, 17 and Pl. 60,1.
275. As the stemmed bowl from Ialysos NT 4:8, *Mee* 1982, Pl. 17,1, Mee considers the bowl to be locally made and emphasizes the rarity of the type.
276. For instance Tiryns 1977, Abb. 50 and Tiryns 1976, Abb. 37,8.
277. *CVA* DK, Pl. 47.6.
278. *Mee* 1982, pp. 65 and 41.
279. *Prehistoric Emporio*, p. 583 (no. 2702).
280. N. K. Sandars, *BSA* 53–54, 1958–1959, p. 235.
281. A. Maiuri, ASAtene 6–7, p. 16, Fig. 15,21. L. Morricone, *ASAtene* NS 27–28, p. 150.
282. O. Höckmann, *JRGZM* 27, 1980, p. 38 ff. It has not been possible to include R.A.J. Avila's recent study (*Präh. Bronzefunde* V,1) in this treatment.
283. G. Jacopi, *ASAtene* 13–14, p. 344 f, no. 3, Fig. 95 and Höckmann cit. F.7.
284. *MV* Tf. D. 16.
285. O. Höckmann cit. p. 120.
286. L. Morricone, *ASAtene* NS 34–35, Figs. 63,65 and 66. Höckmann cit. F21, F22 and F23.
287. L. Morricone, ASAtene NS 34–35, p. 253. Höckmann cit. p. 46 and p. 140. The sword was catalogued by Sandars, *AJA* 67, 1963, p. 145.
288. *Mee* 1982, pp. 61–65.
289. Supra p. 106ff and infra p. 113ff.
290. *Archaeologia Homerica* I. J, "Jagd und Fischfang", pp. 169–175.
291. Both in *OpusAth* 3, 1944.
292. E. Gjerstad cit. p. 92, Fig. 5,4 = Furumark IIIC Fig. 11,15–12,15 and W. Kraiker und K. Kübler, *Kerameikos* I, Tf. 11,503 = E. Gjerstad cit. Fig. 5,5.
293. Cit. p. 244.
294. Characteristic is *Prophitis Elias*, Grave VI,4 – considered by Schachermeyr to be imported from Achaia, *Ägäische Frühzeit* IV, Tf. 39.
295. E. Gjerstad cit. Fig. 1,17 et al. and in general V. Karageorghis, *Alaas, A Protogeometric Necropolis in Cyprus*, Nicosia 1975.
296. See S. Dietz, *Asine* II,1, B. Wells, *Asine* II,IV,2 and B. Santillo Frizell, *Asine* II,3 (Final Mycenaean).
297. Not so much has been published.
298. *AJA* 72, 1968, p. 51 ff., with further references to the pattern.
299. L. Morricone, *ASAtene* NS 27–28, p. 225 ff. The amphoriskos, inv.no. 198, the stirrup jar is depicted on Figs. 242 and 246.
300. *Asine* II,3, no. 40.

119

C. Summary of chronology and foreign relation

301. *MP*, p. 3, note 1.
302. *Chronology*, p. 32.
303. *Chronology*, p. 37.
304. As outlined by C. W. Blegen, A. J. B. Wace, M. Mackeprang and others.
305. I.e. mainly Argive.
306. *Furumark IIIC*, passim.
307. Cit p. 196.
308. See, for instance, the comments by Lisa French in AA 1969, p. 133, V. d'A. Desborough. because of lack of stratigraphical evidence, showed a sound scepticism, but accepted the general theory in *The Last Mycenaeans and their Successors*, Cambridge 1964, p. 5.
309. Cit. p. 208.
310. Cit. p. 211.
311. *French* I-V and E. French, *AA* 1969, pp. 133–136. K. A. Wardle, *BSA* 64, 1969 and *BSA* 68, 1973. *Tiryns* 1976, 1977, 1978 and 1981. For an excellent survey of the evidence, see K. Kilian, *JRGZM* 27, 1980, pp. 166–195 with comprehensive references – also *Ägäische Frühzeit* II and IV passim.
312. M. Popham and E. Milburn, *BSA* 66, 1971, pp. 333–352.
313. J. Rutter in *Symposium on the Dark Ages in Greece*, N.Y. 1977, pp. 1–20 and *Hesperia* 48, pp. 348–392.
314. *Perati* passim.
315. *Tiryns* 1977, p. 409.
316. I am greatly indebted to Professor Kilian for an excellent demonstration of the results of the 1982 excavations, see now *JHS AR* 29, 1983, p. 27.
317. *AA* 1962, p. 222. *Ägäische Frühzeit* II, pp. 249–267.
318. K. A. Wardle, *BSA* 68, 1973, p. 306, Fig. 5.
319. K. A. Wardle, *BSA* 68, 1973, p. 298.
320. *Ägäische Frühzeit* II, p. 266.
321. E. S. Sherratt, *BSA* 75, 1980, p. 199 ff.
321a. Such a development must at any rate be gradual. I am greatly indebted to Professor Klaus Kilian from whom I received a manuscript for a lecture delivered in Heidelberg (to be published in *Akad. Heidelberg Jb.* 1981). From this manuscript it appear, that a great change in settlement pattern in the Argolid occurs between the phases LH IIIB2 and LH IIIC (Compare Fig. 2 with Fig. 3 in the cited article).
322. D.U. Schilardi, in J. L. Davis and J. F. Cherry (eds.), *Papers in Cycladic Prehistory*, 1979, p. 158 ff. and early IIIC, supra note 189 and R. Barber, *BSA* 76, 1981, p. 11.
323. R. Barber, *BSA* 76, 1981, p. 11.
324. R. Barber, cit.
325. J. Rutter in *Symposium on the Dark Ages in Greece*, N.Y. 1977, p. 3.
326. *BSA* 66, 1971, pp. 333–352, passim.
327. *Tiryns* 1981, passim, and earlier published reports on the excavations in Tiryns, Unterburg.
328. S. Dietz, *Asine* II,1 and B. Wells, *Asine* II,4,1 passim.
329. See for instance, V. Hankey and P. Warren *BICS* 21, p. 148 – with references.
330. For a recent survey see V. Karageorghis, *Cyprus, from the Stone Age to the Romans*, Nicosia 1982. E. S. Sherratt, *BSA* 75, 1980, p. 195 ff.
331. M. Popham, *Acts Nicosia* 1978, p. 190.
332. *Ägäische Frühzeit* II, p. 277 ff.
333. *Mee* 1982.
334. *CVA* DK – as pointed out supra not even this type of kylix may indicate a dating in early LH IIIB.
335. The deep bowl no. 1 from Apsaktiras might well be later, supra p. 105.
336. Most recently in *Mee* 1982, p. 88.
337. *Mee* 1982, pp. 65–66. R. Hope Simpson and J. Lazenby, *BSA* 68, 1973, p. 147f.
338. R. E. Jones and C. Mee, *JFA* 5, p. 468.
339. Not least in *Stubbings Levant*, passim.
340. C. Mee, *The Dodecanese in the Bronze Age*, 1975.
341. *Mee* 1982, p. 88.
342. For the most recent evidence see *Tiryns* 1978/79, p. 170 and Abb. 40,5 and note 69.
343. G. Bass, *Cape Gelidonya : A Bronze Age Ship-wreck*, Philadelphia 1967 p. 165 et passim.
344. Cit p. 469. On the presence of LH IIIB2 sherds in Troy, see P. Åström, *OpusAth*, XIII : 3, 1980, pp. 23–28.
345. Cit. p. 469.
346. *Mee* 1982, p. 89.
347. *Mee* 1982, p. 90.
348. Chr. Podzuweit, *Südosteuropa zwischen 1600 und 1000 v.Chr..*, Berlin 1982, passim.
349. *Tiryns* 1981, pp. 400—401.
350. V. R. d'A. Desborough, *The Greek Dark Ages*, London 1972, p. 49ff, S. Dietz, *Asine* II,1, p. 60. B. Wells, *Asine* II,4,2 passim and Th. J. Papadopoulos, *AA* 1980, p. 166 ff for Achaea.